Professor Ian Lowe AO is emeritus professor of science, technology and society at Griffith University in Brisbane, as well as being an adjunct professor at Sunshine Coast University and Flinders University. His previous books include *A Big Fix*, *Living in the Hothouse*, *A Voice of Reason: Reflections on Australia* and *Bigger or Better? Australia's Population Debate*. Professor Lowe has been a referee for the Intergovernmental Panel on Climate Change, the International Geosphere-Biosphere Programme and the Millennium Assessment. He attended the Geneva, Kyoto and Copenhagen conferences of the parties to the Framework Convention on Climate Change. He was a member of the Australian delegation to the 1999 UNESCO World Conference on Science and has served on many advisory bodies to all levels of government. He was president of the Australian Conservation Foundation (ACF) from 2004 to 2014, and in 2009 the International Academy of Sciences, Health and Ecology awarded him the Konrad Lorenz Gold Medal. He is a fellow of the Australian Academy of Technology and Engineering.

THE LUCKY COUNTRY?

REINVENTING AUSTRALIA

IAN LOWE

uqp

First published in 2016 by University of Queensland Press
PO Box 6042, St Lucia, Queensland 4067 Australia

www.uqp.com.au
uqp@uqp.uq.edu.au

© 2016 Ian Lowe

This book is copyright. Except for private study, research, criticism or reviews, as permitted under the Copyright Act, no part of this book may be reproduced, stored in a retrieval system, or transmitted in any form or by any means without prior written permission. Enquiries should be made to the publisher.

Cover design: Design by Committee
Cover photographs: coal mine by Ladiras / Bigstock; Sydney by Xolct / Bigstock; rainforest by Gevision / Bigstock
Typeset in 12/16 Bembo Std Regular by Post Pre-press Group, Brisbane
Printed in Australia by McPherson's Printing Group, Melbourne

Extracts from *The Lucky Country* by Donald Horne, fifth edition, Penguin, Melbourne, 1998 reproduced with permission by Penguin Australia Pty Ltd.

All attempts have been made to contact copyright licensees for permission to reproduce material. If you believe material for which you hold the rights is reprinted here, please contact the publisher.

Cataloguing-in-Publication entry is available from the
National Library of Australia
http://catalogue.nla.gov.au/

ISBN 978 0 7022 5367 6 (pbk)
ISBN 978 0 7022 5545 8 (epdf)
ISBN 978 0 7022 5546 5 (epub)
ISBN 978 0 7022 5547 2 (kindle)

University of Queensland Press uses papers that are natural, renewable and recyclable products made from wood grown in sustainable forests. The logging and manufacturing processes conform to the environmental regulations of the country of origin.

For Maven Cordelia and all of her generation

CONTENTS

Introduction	1
Environment	9
Geography	57
Society	85
Economy	133
Balance	203
Acknowledgements	233
Sources	235

INTRODUCTION

In his iconic 1964 book, Donald Horne described Australia as 'a lucky country run mainly by second-rate people who share its luck'. He went on to say that we 'live on other people's ideas' and that 'most of our leaders (in all fields) so lack curiosity about the events that surround them that they are often taken by surprise'. His book caused a sensation at the time and became a runaway bestseller. The striking cover, an Albert Tucker painting of a sun-bronzed Aussie, appealed to the traditional Australian image of a country defined by its rural lands and their produce. The phrase 'the lucky country' quickly became part of the language, though its message was often misrepresented by people who had not even read the book, or had skimmed quickly through it and missed the irony of the title.

Donald Horne was a remarkable Australian. He grew up in a country town, but he moved with his parents to Sydney while he was at school. He began to study at the University of Sydney with the intention of becoming a teacher, but his formal education was interrupted when he was conscripted into the army during World War II. After the war he drifted through a brief dalliance with the diplomatic service into a career as a journalist, rising through the ranks to edit magazines. When it was rumoured that he was about to be sacked from the editorship of *The Bulletin*, then a popular publication, the University of New South Wales offered him a post in its Faculty of Arts. He became a prominent academic in the politics department, achieving the distinction of being promoted to professor without even having a bachelor's degree! A few months before he died in 2005, the University of Sydney finally conferred an honorary Doctor of Letters on the man who was probably their most famous drop-out. Glyn Davis, now vice-chancellor of Melbourne University, who as an honours student was supervised by Horne, described him as 'a familiar public intellectual in Australia, a man who helped the nation understand itself'. Davis observed that *The Lucky Country* 'was both description and program ... calling for government to encourage the innovation missing from public and business life'. It resonated with the community because it was such a perceptive analysis of what is good about Australia, as well as what we could do better. Davis attributed the breadth of Horne's understanding of Australia to the many roles he had filled: 'student, soldier, diplomatic cadet, young journalist, editor, advertising executive, academic'. He was truly a unique individual.

Reflecting on the book's reception 35 years after it was first published, Horne wrote about the way his argument had been misunderstood or deliberately misrepresented. He said, 'misuse of the phrase "the lucky country", as if it were praise for Australia rather than a warning, has been a tribute to the empty-mindedness of a mob of assorted public wafflers. When the book first came out, people had no doubt the phrase was ironic. Twisting it around to mean the opposite of what was intended has silenced the three loud warnings in the book about the future of Australia.' The first of these three loud warnings was that it is essential to accept the challenges of where Australia

Introduction

sits on the map. These challenges include how we develop relationships with our Asian neighbours, with whom we have tended to engage on purely economic terms; how we reconcile our colonial history of dispossessing Australia's original inhabitants; and how we develop our foreign policy and defence strategies in the complex world of the Asia–Pacific, recognising the competing interests of the two great powers, China and the USA, as well as a significant group of middleweights like ourselves. Horne's second warning was the need for 'a bold redefinition of what the whole place adds up to now', which requires us to recognise that Australia has changed fundamentally in recent decades and have a serious public discussion about societal values, population growth and what kind of country we'd like to become. Obviously that process would be facilitated if we were to elect visionary leaders who were willing and able to guide, or at least participate in, the public discussion. His third warning saw a need for a revolution in economic priorities, 'especially by investing in education and science', which have been sacrificed in this country to privilege markets and the pursuit of endless growth, while we further tether ourselves to a globalised economy that puts our well-being in the hands of forces we can't control.

Writing in 1998, Horne observed that these same three warnings should be repeated, 'with the amplifying knob turned up'. If he were alive today, he would certainly think that the three warnings are still valid, more than 50 years after he originally issued them. In this book, I revisit these warnings to show you why they are still relevant today; if anything, they are more urgent because they have been neglected for 50 years by politicians content to drift with the random tides of international affairs. I am also compelled to add a warning of my own: the environmental challenges we face simply can no longer be ignored. Horne's three warnings – on geography, society and the economy – must all be filtered through the lens of our precarious environmental situation. The devastatingly extreme weather patterns that come with climate change, the loss of biodiversity, the breakdown of the Earth's ecosystems and our unsustainable use of finite resources all affect our future prospects.

In 2015, the need for change was signalled by a UN report on progress toward sustainability. It showed that Australia ranks 18th out of the 34 Organisation for Economic Co-operation and Development (OECD) countries: below the UK, New Zealand and well below Canada. The rating was based on 34 indicators covering economic, social and environmental progress. Australia ranked among the worst of all the affluent countries on such indicators as our level of resource use, the municipal waste we generate, the greenhouse gases we use for each unit of economic output and our obesity rate. We were also well below the average on social indicators such as the level of education we reach, the gender pay difference and percentage of women in parliament, economic indicators such as the poverty rate and the degree of inequality, as well as environmental indicators such as how much land we protect and our share of renewable energy. Perhaps most worrying, we are also well below average in our capacity to monitor progress toward the Sustainable Development Goals. As the old adage goes, you can't manage what you don't measure.

While the global future looks extremely problematic, Australia has unique advantages that would allow us to be both a model for the developed world and a beacon of hope for the developing nations in our region. It will not be easy. What Horne acerbically called 'empty-minded public wafflers' remain an obstacle to achieving that desirable future, as do powerful

Introduction

vested interests and their political clients. Yet I am an incurable optimist and believe that the changes are possible; as the author Arundhati Roy enthusiastically expressed it, a new world is not just possible, but its early beginnings are already visible to the prepared senses: 'on a quiet day, I can hear her breathing'. Like a small plant emerging from the earth, this new world needs to be nurtured – but the mighty Moreton Bay fig trees that are such an iconic part of the Queensland landscape were once tiny saplings. We must cultivate those seeds of change so we can grow to become a truly lucky country. That will be a wonderful legacy to future generations.

Let me tell you something of the background I bring to this book. That is important for you to know because I, like you and everyone else, see the world through the lenses of my values and my experience. Like Donald Horne, I grew up in small country towns. I was lucky to get a state bursary when I finished primary school, enabling my parents to send me to the state high school about 40 kilometres away and get a very good education. After finishing school, I got a job in Sydney working for a company that built electronic equipment; they supported me to study electrical engineering part-time at the new university of tecÿology. Four years later, that institution had become the University of New South Wales and I moved to a job in its applied physics department, building equipment for researchers. Like Horne, I also learned to write by contributing to the student newspaper. I became heavily involved in student politics and in the years after *The Lucky Country* was published, I was active in the debates it stimulated about our geographic position, our responsibility for the treatment of the original Australians, our investment in education and science, and our rapidly changing urban societies. Unlike Horne, I was not moved by his arguments to support the American War in Vietnam.

After graduating, I had the rewarding experience of ten weeks travelling around the USA with a group of 'student leaders' from nine other countries, meeting politicians and other decision-makers. A creative rearrangement of my return fare allowed me to visit Japan, Taiwan, Hong Kong, Singapore and the Philippines on my way home, giving me a wonderful introduction to the variety and complexity of our region. I taught high school science for eighteen months, then went to the UK to research for a doctorate in physics at the University of York. Ironically, given where my thinking has moved since then, my doctoral research was funded by the UK Atomic Energy Authority! My first academic post was in the TecÿOlogy Faculty at the then new UK Open University. It involved working in multi-disciplinary teams to produce integrated learning experiences for mature-age students. After the publication of *The Limits to Growth* and the subsequent oil crisis in the 1970s, I became very interested in the issues arising from energy supply and use. I returned to Australia in 1980 to lecture in science, tecÿOlogy and society and direct the Science Policy Research Centre at Griffith University in Brisbane.

As well as my academic work, I have been involved in a wide range of advisory roles to all levels of government, mostly in the broad areas of energy and environment. I directed our Commission for the Future in 1988, when we published an excellent discussion paper written by Donald Horne, arguing persuasively for government support for innovation. I chaired the advisory council that produced the first independent national report on the state of the environment in 1996. As the science we drew together showed clearly that we are not living sustainably, I became active in public discussion of the environmental problems. I negotiated early retirement from Griffith University at the end of 1999 and the university subsequently

Introduction

made me an emeritus professor, which is an honorary appointment for life. This freed me to be more involved in other activities and led to me being invited to be president of the Australian Conservation Foundation, a role I filled from 2004 to 2014. I have given four addresses to the National Press Club about the need to change our approach and become an innovative society, in charge of our own destiny and working purposefully for a sustainable future.

Those of us who were born around the middle of last century in Australia were incredibly lucky in the lottery of life. We grew up in a time of peace and relative plenty in a secure country. But we need to recognise that there are now storm clouds on the horizon. We have a responsibility to future generations, our own descendants, to be thinking about our legacy to them. As I was writing this book, I became a grandfather for the first time. Looking at my precious little grand-daughter, I could not help reflecting on what sort of world she will grow up in. She could well live until the end of this century. I hope that we will act responsibly by putting in place the structures and policies that will allow her to have a secure, comfortable and rewarding life. So I have dedicated this book to her, and all of her generation of young Australians.

I have assumed that you, the reader, are a thoughtful Australian who shares my view that we should be thinking about the future we are all creating. In this introduction, I have briefly set out the warnings Donald Horne sounded 50 years ago. In the following four sections, I will summarise what I believe to be the current situation and prospects for change in each of the key areas in turn: environment, geography, society and economy. Then I will conclude with some thoughts about combining these aspects of our life to shape a future that could be sustainable.

I hope the discussion will help you in two ways. First, I believe we all need to understand how our individual actions can contribute to shaping a better future. Second, and more importantly, I believe we all need to be putting pressure on our elected representatives at all levels – local, state or territory, and national – to be acting more responsibly, taking the decisions and setting the structures now that will enable us as citizens to play our part in creating a genuinely lucky country.

ENVIRONMENT

Australia has some very serious environmental problems. If we are to achieve our goal of ecological sustainability, these problems need to be dealt with immediately ... The problems are the cumulative consequences of population growth and distribution, lifestyles, technologies and demands on natural resources ... No single government or sector is to blame for these problems. We are all responsible.
—Australia: State of the Environment 1996

Much of Australia's environment and heritage is in good shape, or improving. Other parts are in poor condition or deteriorating ... Our changing climate, and growing population and economy, are now confronting us with new challenges.
—Australia: State of the Environment 2011

The current observed changes to the Earth systems are unprecedented in human history ... several critical global, regional or local thresholds are close or have been exceeded ... abrupt and possibly irreversible changes to the life support functions of the planet are likely to occur.
—GEO5, UNEP 2012

The first edition of Donald Horne's *The Lucky Country* says absolutely nothing about environmental issues, because they were not on the radar in 1964. Most observers see the 1962 US publication of *Silent Spring* by Rachel Carson – which set out the detrimental effects of pesticides on birds, animals and the world's food supply – as the beginning of broad awareness of the impacts of human activity on natural systems. It began a discussion of these issues among scientists and the more aware public officials. The first laws seeking to protect environmental standards emerged about ten years later. Of course, there had always been a link between industrial production and local pollution, as recognised in the old Yorkshire saying 'where there's muck, there's brass' – wherever there is a mess, it is the result of somebody making money. The problem that has developed in the last 50 years is that our growing human numbers and increasing consumption have dramatically increased the scale of environmental effects: from the local to the regional and now the global. Our ecosystem is under serious threat – from climate change and other effects of human activity – and our political efforts at regulating these threats have been seriously compromised by those with economic interests in maintaining the damaging behaviour. These issues clash most strongly in the areas of energy use and resource exports, and the strain that population growth puts on our urban development and infrastructure. Shifting our development trajectory onto a path that could be sustainable will require a concerted effort by our politicians to act in the interest of future generations. It will also need all of us to accept less wasteful living standards.

THE DAMAGE WE'RE DOING

Twenty years ago, the United Nations Environment Programme (UNEP) decided to develop reports on the *Global Environmental Outlook (GEO)*. I was in a workshop UNEP convened to discuss the structure of these reports. Five have now been issued, each one expressing the need for change more urgently than the previous study. As long ago as 1999, the second *GEO* report warned that serious problems were emerging from increasing human consumption of resources. It concluded that the standard development model, assuming continuing growth in material living standards everywhere in the world, was not sustainable and 'doing nothing is no longer an option'. World leaders essentially ignored that clarion call. As subsequent reports have pointed out, the global environmental problems are steadily worsening, arguably the inevitable consequence of the continually growing population and increasing consumption per person. One recent report, *GEO5*, said in 2012 that despite efforts to 'slow the rate or extent of change', neither the scope nor speed of these adverse changes has abated in the past five years. We are now close to or exceeding the thresholds of 'possibly irreversible changes to the life-support functions of the planet'. An abrupt and irreversible example is the accelerated melting of the Arctic ice sheet due to global warming.

GEO5 noted that such changes are already having serious consequences for human well-being. Droughts are combining with socio-economic pressures to affect food production and human security. Increasing average temperatures have led to significant human health problems such as increased outbreaks of malaria. Increased frequency and severity of climatic events, such as floods and droughts, are affecting both human settlements and the natural world. Rising sea levels pose a threat to coastal buildings as well as reducing the capacity of some small island developing states in the Pacific to produce their food. Perhaps most importantly, biodiversity loss affects everything from our food supply to the loss of existing and possible future medicines from natural systems.

If we want to avoid these consequences, we need to recognise and respond to the root causes of the environmental problems, rather than concentrating just on the symptoms. As one obvious example, it is not enough to reduce *individual* impacts on natural systems; we need to reduce the *total* impact. The ecosystem does not recognise or respond to the number of humans on Earth or the scale of our industrial production, but it does respond to the sum total of our water extraction, our food production, our dumping of wastes, our destruction of habitat and our release of introduced species. There is no prospect, even in principle, of a sustainable future unless we recognise and respond to that fundamental truth. It calls into question the underlying assumption of most decision-makers, the myth that continuing growth is both possible and desirable. This is 'a toxic meme' which makes it impossible to have a rational discussion about the problems we face.

Climate change

The atmospheric concentration of the most important greenhouse gas, carbon dioxide, has varied over the period of human existence between about 180 and 280 parts per million. It is now over 400 parts per million and still increasing rapidly. This has already resulted in significant changes: the global average temperature has increased by nearly a degree, sea levels have risen, glaciers have retreated, rainfall patterns have changed and we are seeing more frequent extreme events: longer and worse droughts, heavy rainfall events, catastrophic bushfires and more intense tropical storms. Perth's average annual run-off into its water supply system is now about one-third of what it was between 1910 and 1975. The ability of its residents to continue to water lawns and gardens is being maintained only by using desalination plants which process Indian Ocean water.

The Australian Academy of Science recently advised that global emissions of greenhouse gases need to peak by 2020 and then be reduced sharply to have a 50 per cent chance of avoiding the Plimsoll Line of 2 degrees increase in average global temperature, the level beyond which our ability to adapt becomes problematic. Such an increase in *average* temperatures would see it get much hotter in inland Australia, so the Commonwealth Scientific and Industrial Research Organisation (CSIRO) has shown our food production would be severely affected during my grand-daughter's lifetime. At the global level, scientists worry that beyond the 2 degree increase we are likely to see an unstoppable momentum toward such changes as destabilising major ice sheets, causing sea levels to rise several metres. That shows how seriously we should be taking the issue of climate change. We need an unprecedented level of international cooperation and willingness to invest in clean energy systems to achieve reductions on the scale required.

Biodiversity

The loss of the Earth's biological diversity is permanent. Extinct species do not return. (At least, that is true of our present tecÿology. Optimists think it might be possible to bring back the thylacine or the woolly mammoth from DNA in the preserved bodies of these extinct creatures, but that capacity is certainly not proven.) The World Wide Fund for Nature (WWF) and the Global Footprint Network, in the *Living Planet Report 2014*, reviewed some 10,000 species of mammals, reptiles, birds, fish and amphibians, and found that, on average, populations have declined by more than 50 per cent since 1970. The current rate of species loss was shown by the UN's *Millennium Assessment* report to be comparable with those during the previous great extinction episodes of the Earth's history. That study gloomily concluded that we could lose up to a third of all mammal, bird and amphibian species this century if present trends continue. That is not a minor blip, but a catastrophic loss of the planet's biodiversity. We cannot predict the consequences, but we do know that when a species disappears there are effects up and down the food chain; species on which it preys increase in numbers, while species that relied on it for food decline. We are pulling random rocks out of the wall of life, without being aware of when whole sections might collapse.

We know what is causing the decline and loss of species: the loss of habitat, introduced species and chemical pollution. All those forces are driven by growing human population numbers and increasing average consumption, causing us to make ever greater demands on natural systems. The *Living Planet Report* estimated that we are now using about 150 per cent of the sustainable productivity of natural systems. While there might be an economic case for deficit budgets in the short term, especially if the borrowing is used to invest in the capacity of future generations to have a good life, there is absolutely no ecological case for the present approach of systematically running down our natural capital. Our descendants will suffer terribly if we continue to disregard our reliance on natural systems and the wonderful biological diversity of the Earth.

Climate change adds an extra pressure to these three driving forces causing the loss of biodiversity; not just by increasing average temperatures but also by altering rainfall patterns, shrinking terrestrial glaciers and Arctic sea-ice, raising the sea level and causing more frequent and severe extreme events. Some animal species can move as the climate changes, and shifts of that kind have been well documented in recent years, but others are trapped on shrinking islands of acceptable habitat. Plant species are obviously less able to move in response to changing climate. That means the overall outlook is quite bleak unless we change our approach to natural systems.

PLAYING POLITICS WITH THE EARTH

Scientists started sounding warnings about our impacts on natural systems in the 1960s. In Australia, a group convened a meeting in Canberra which led to the establishment in 1965 of the Australian Conservation Foundation. The first modest step to change behaviour in the right direction was the national environmental legislation signed into law in 1969 by US president Richard Nixon. A response to the concerns arising from *Silent Spring*, it set limits on the release of some pollutants into the environment.

The Whitlam government introduced our first environmental law in Australia only five years later in 1974 and appointed Dr Moss Cass as minister. A medico before he went into politics, Cass was the driving force introducing environmental impact assessment for major developments such as the proposed Ranger uranium mine in the Northern Territory.

ENVIRONMENT

The subsequent Fraser government also used other legal powers for environmental protection. The Bjelke-Petersen government in Queensland was enthusiastic to permit sand mining on Fraser Island, but the proposal collapsed in the early 1980s when the Fraser government in Canberra refused to grant export permits for the minerals that would have been produced. That decision by the Commonwealth government set the stage for critical environmental struggles in Tasmania.

By the 1980s, most states had some form of environmental law requiring major property developments to be assessed for their possible environmental impacts. These assessments have often identified potential problems that could be ameliorated by modifying the proposed activities, and there is no doubt that improvements have been achieved. Critics point out that those proposing a development commission the assessment and, not surprisingly, almost all these 'independent' assessments recommend that the development should proceed, sometimes in modified form but often as originally proposed. From time to time, angry local community groups challenge these assessments in the courts; in a celebrated 2015 case, Commonwealth minister Greg Hunt conceded that due process had not been followed in his approval of the proposed Carmichael coal mine in central Queensland. While community groups generally feel that courts are not sympathetic to their arguments, the ability to challenge approvals is an important safeguard that some business interests and politicians would like to see curbed. The underlying problem is that governments generally think that environmental protection is less important than economic development, so even environment departments often behave as if their job was to reassure the public that the impacts of proposed developments should be tolerated.

Greenies in Tasmania

In the 1970s, the Tasmanian government proposed a new reservoir for hydro-electric development that would flood Lake Pedder, an iconic site long revered by bushwalkers. There were large-scale protests but the government of 'Electric Eric' Reece was determined to go ahead with the scheme. The flooding of Lake Pedder led directly to the formation of the United Tasmania Group, recognised as the world's first green party. It unsuccessfully ran candidates in state elections. Their actions in turn saw the election a decade later of the first 'Green Independent' politicians and the subsequent formation of the Australian Greens, now a significant third force in Australian politics, as discussed further below. In many ways, the Lake Pedder struggle was the overture to the consequent major drama, the proposal to dam the Franklin River.

In the late 1970s, the Tasmanian government proposed another addition to its hydro-electric system, based on the Gordon-below-Franklin dam. Environmentalists were outraged by the threat to this iconic wild river. A striking photograph of a rock island bend became the focus of a concerted campaign to stop the damming of the river, including a blockade of the site by a group of determined activists. A Tasmanian GP, Dr Bob Brown, was a prominent leader of the campaign; he was subsequently elected to the Tasmanian parliament and then the Australian Senate. The state government responded to the campaign by describing the Franklin as a 'leech-ridden ditch' and held a vote to try to show it had a public mandate for the project, offering voters a choice between two alternative sites for the dam. An amazing 33 per cent wrote 'NO DAMS' on their ballot papers. This spurred conservationists on the mainland to urge voters in a by-election for the federal electorate of Flinders to follow suit and write that message on their ballot papers. When 41 per cent did, it sent a clear signal to politicians that this was an issue of importance.

That action probably emboldened Bob Hawke, as leader of the ALP opposition going into the 1983 election, to promise 'The dam will not be built', although it was not clear that a national government had the power to stop the Tasmanian administration from its proposed action. Having swept to power, the Hawke government legislated to stop the dam. The Tasmanian government took its case to the High Court, arguing that the Constitution did not give the national government power to protect the environment or regulate the electricity industry. The Commonwealth argued that it was exercising its constitutional power to enter into treaties: having signed the UN's Treaty for the Protection of Biodiversity, it was arguably required to overrule state governments when necessary to protect threatened ecological systems. In a judgment that changed forever the legal basis of environmental protection in Australia, the High Court decided by the knife-edge margin of five judges to four that the Commonwealth did have the power to intervene. The project was stopped; the Franklin River remains a magnificent fast-flowing stream.

Global reporting

In 1987 the World Commission on Environment and Development, chaired by the Norwegian prime minister, Gro Harlem Brundtland, released a report titled *Our Common Future*. The report set out the conditions for sustainable development, calling for the integration of economic and environmental policies to achieve this goal. The Hawke government responded by creating nine working groups to examine how Australia could achieve ecologically sustainable development in specific areas such as manufacturing, mining, agriculture, forestry, transport, energy supply and so on. I was a member of the working group on energy use and was struck by the broad agreement among a very diverse group including industrialists, farmers, Indigenous people, consumer representatives, trade unionists and environmentalists. The only serious dissenters were Commonwealth public servants, mostly trained in economics and consequently devout adherents to the belief that the market would deliver better outcomes than concerted government policies. These bureaucrats heavily edited the working group's recommendations, but they still amounted to a program of serious action to take social and environmental factors into account when considering proposed economic developments. The published compendium of policy ideas is listed in the 'Sources' section at the end of this book; they would still amount to progressive change if they were to be implemented today! When I looked back over the recommendations of the group I was in, we thought 25 years ago the government should study the relative benefits and costs of a carbon tax versus an emissions trading scheme, that energy utilities should invest in cost-effective measures to reduce energy use by improving appliance efficiency, that the benefits of retrofitting insulation to rental housing should be assessed, that appliances should be labelled to indicate their efficiency and standards should be lifted, that waste disposal should be reviewed to reduce energy use and greenhouse gas released, and that governments should invest in research to improve both renewable energy supply tecÿologies and the efficiency of turning energy into the services people want.

    The process culminated in the Council of Australian Governments (COAG) adopting in December 1992 the National Strategy for Ecologically Sustainable Development (NSESD). In principle, this committed the Commonwealth and all state and territory governments to make their economic development socially and ecologically sustainable. The recently removed government led by Campbell Newman in Queensland and the Abbott government in Canberra showed few signs of recognising this legal commitment as they pushed ahead with any proposal that might grow the economy, even new export coal mines. Among the provisions of the NSESD are the needs to recognise our international responsibilities, to maintain the integrity of ecological systems and to prevent further loss of our unique biodiversity. The most fundamental point is that our approach to economic development should not reduce the opportunities available to future generations, but much of the decision-making in Australia does just this because it is still, as Donald Horne lamented 50 years ago, largely driven by short-term thinking.

Also in 1992 the Australian government attended the Rio Earth Summit, which agreed that national governments should produce regular reports on the state of the environment. In 1994 I was appointed to chair the advisory council charged with preparing the first such report. The advisory body was made up of a diverse and extremely knowledgeable group of people: scientists and other academics, business leaders, consultants, a trade union official, an Indigenous elder, an agribusiness adviser and farmer, an environmentalist and an information expert. Our work was guided by seven expert groups who compiled reports on specific aspects of our environment such as inland rivers. The Keating ALP government set up the council and successive ministers gave us free rein to report honestly; Senator JoŸ Faulkner said at a formal launch of the process that he wanted 'the full picture, the good, the bad and the ugly' so nobody could avoid responsibility. It was not to be a government report, sanitised to put those in power in a good light; it was to be a report *to* government by a truly independent advisory body.

When it appeared likely that there would be a change of government in the 1996 election, we worked round the clock to ensure that the report went to the printers before the election; we worried that an incoming Coalition administration might have wanted to rein in the process rather than receive a genuinely independent report. I actually signed off on the page proofs the day before the election and sent the caretaker minister a fax that night, telling him the report was in the hands of the printers. The Howard government was elected the next day, so they were in power when our report was published and released. We said that much of Australia's environment was in good condition by international standards, but some serious problems needed addressing to achieve the goal of living sustainably: loss of our unique biodiversity, the state of our inland rivers, degradation of large areas of our productive land, the pressures on the coastal zone and rapidly increasing release of the greenhouse gases causing climate change. These problems did not have simple causes that could be attributed to any productive sector or any level of government. They were, we said, the consequence of the scale and growth of our population, our consumption patterns, our lifestyle choices and the tecÿologies we use. The final section of the report, 'Towards Ecological Sustainability', showed that living sustainably would require making our economic and social decisions within the context of their environmental impacts.

Political value judgments

The advisory council's terms of reference did not allow us to make any recommendations for dealing with the problems we identified. Some observers thought that was a weakness of the process, but I saw it as a good approach. An objective assessment can determine if there are environmental problems and identify causes, but proposing solutions inevitably involves political judgments. As a concrete example, if an environmental assessment were to show that urban air quality was unacceptable and the root cause was motor vehicle emissions, a range of responses would be possible. The number of vehicles on the roads could be curtailed or the average pollution per vehicle could be reduced. Either of those goals could be achieved by financial measures such as road tolls or registration charges related to fuel efficiency, by regulatory measures such as mandated efficiency improvements or restrictions on the right to drive into central areas, or by some form of community education. An independent advisory body could spell out a range of alternatives, but elected politicians have to make the value judgments about the cost and benefits of alternative approaches.

This point had been made a few years earlier by the outcome of a major environmental and social dispute. Before the 1989 election, the North Broken Hill mining company proposed a gold and palladium mine at Coronation Hill in the Northern Territory. It claimed that the mine would bring economic benefits and provide jobs in an area of high unemployment, but environmentalists said it would risk polluting water that runs into Kakadu National Park. Local Indigenous people were also unhappy that the mine would damage sacred sites and offend their spiritual values. The Hawke government faced a dilemma: approving the mine would probably cost their party the preferences of Green voters, which it would need to get re-elected, but refusing the application would allow the Coalition opposition to brand his government as economically irresponsible. Their solution was to defer a decision, promising to set up a new body to make detailed assessments of such proposals and report to government.

When he was returned to power, Hawke set up the Resources Assessment Commission and charged it with considering the

Coronation Hill proposal as its first task. The commission did a detailed study of the proposed mine and produced a major report, but not in the form the government had anticipated. It set out the range of credible studies of the economic benefits of the mine. It analysed the social benefits, primarily the new employment opportunities, and the social costs and the impact on the spiritual values of the Indigenous people. It also estimated the environmental risks of the project. It then said that deciding if the economic and social benefits outweighed the social costs and environmental risks was a value judgment that could be made only by elected representatives. The Cabinet was divided on the issue and clearly uncomfortable with being forced to make that collective value judgment. Eventually, after a bitter debate, Hawke's view that the costs did not justify the benefits prevailed, but discontent with that outcome was a major factor when the ALP caucus voted shortly afterwards for Paul Keating to take over from Hawke as their leader and prime minister. Keating's discomfort with the process led him to abolish the commission, returning to a system in which the political value judgments are covert rather than out in the open. That was consistent with his government's approach to reporting on the state of the environment. The expert advisory group reviewed the evidence and set out the problems without being allowed to suggest any policy responses.

Since the 1996 release of that first report on the state of the national environment, there have been three subsequent reports at five-year intervals. All these reports identified the same serious problems. All said that they are still getting worse. That overall perspective has been confirmed by the Australian Bureau of Statistics, which has collected time-series data since 1990 in the broad areas of economic development, social change and environmental change. The first report in the early twenty-first century showed that all the economic indicators had improved throughout the 1990s, while the social indicators had been mixed — some better, some worse — and all the environmental indicators had got worse. The same pattern has emerged in subsequent reports. Any objective analysis would conclude that our environmental laws, while they are undoubtedly having some effects, are not achieving their stated goal. Our recent economic development has come at some social cost and at considerable cost to our natural environment.

Despite this, in recent years Coalition governments at national and state level have launched an attack on what they denigrate as 'green tape'. They claim that needless concern about possible environmental problems is holding back desirable economic developments. As well as watering down the requirements for environmental assessment, the Coalition has also withdrawn the funding of Environmental Defenders Offices, which have provided legal advice to community groups concerned about the environmental impacts of proposed major developments and sometimes assisted them with legal challenges.

In 2015, the UN Educational, Scientific and Cultural Organization (UNESCO) considered taking the unprecedented step of listing the Great Barrier Reef as being World Heritage 'in danger', given that half of the reef systems' coral cover has been lost in the last 50 years. There is no one simple cause, as the *State of the Environment* reports have said. The reef systems have been badly affected by run-off of nutrients and sediment from the mainland, itself a consequence of increasing agricultural production to meet the needs of a growing population. The reef systems have also been affected by climate change, by severe tropical cyclones and by predators like the crown-of-thorns starfish, an indicator the ecological systems have been significantly perturbed.

Australia's main political concern was not the embarrassment that an affluent country was unable to look after the world's greatest coral reef systems, but that a negative report from the UNESCO committee might affect the tourism industry! After frantic lobbying by Queensland and Australian governments, including hard work by embassies around the world putting pressure on countries on the relevant UNESCO committee, that body pulled back from listing the Great Barrier Reef as in danger. It did, however, put Australia on notice that we will be shamed on the global stage if it doesn't meet two targets. UNESCO wants to see measurable movement toward implementing the stated reef plan by the end of 2016. More importantly, it wants to see improvements made in the direct measures of reef health like coral cover, as well as the driving forces like poor water quality and over-fishing, by 2019. Since both Commonwealth and state governments have been much better at bold symbolic announcements than doing the hard yards of implementing policy, especially when that involves tackling short-term commercial interests, the future of the Great Barrier Reef looks very grim.

When it comes to our native vegetation, some politicians have a crass utilitarian approach that sees a tree as only being valuable if it is cut down and turned into products for sale. *The Rise and Fall of Gunns Ltd* by Quentin Beresford shows in shocking detail how successive governments in Tasmania were happy to see old-growth temperate forests clear-felled to produce low-value woodchips for export to overseas pulp mills. No leader questioned the value of the habitat, the impact on air and water quality of having forests, or their aesthetic and spiritual value to the community. There was little consideration even of the alternative economic benefits of the tourist income that might be produced by the attractiveness of pristine forests.

When the Goss government in Queensland conducted an inquiry into logging on Fraser Island, it found that the industry was not sustainably using the forest on that unique sand island; logging was subsequently phased out. After the Howard government introduced Regional Forest Agreements, which were seen in some states as providing a continuing licence to destroy woodland, the Beattie government in Queensland brought together the timber industry, environmentalists and regulators to agree on a process for transition. It involved an end to logging forests of high conservation value and a substantial investment in plantations to meet timber needs. That should be a model for our future use of forests. Unfortunately, the Bligh government felt obliged to sell public assets in its desperate attempt to meet the needs of the rapidly growing urban population, so it leased the rights to the plantation timber to a foreign company. I can't imagine that company having the same interest in the long-term management of the forests as was shown by the former Queensland Forestry Corporation – but I should admit that I am a biased observer, as I was on the board of that corporation.

These are specific examples of the general tendency to see politics as synonymous with economic management, assuming that social and environmental problems can always be solved if the economy is booming. Of course, it is more difficult to solve other problems at the same time as coping with economic recession, but the 1987 report of the World Commission on Environment and Development made clear that economic progress must be built on sound environmental foundations.

The ozone hole: an optimistic yet cautionary tale

Let's be optimistic for a moment. The example of ozone depletion shows that it is possible, if the need is seen as being sufficiently urgent, for the world to agree to solve a critical environmental problem. Scientific studies showed in 1972 that the release of chlorofluorocarbons (CFCs) into the atmosphere would deplete the ozone layer, exposing us and all natural systems to increased levels of ultraviolet radiation. But the industry that sold CFCs resisted change by denying what these studies had proven, in just the same way as the tobacco industry had denied the link between smoking and lung cancer. Reviewing the debate in *The Ozone War* in 1979, Dotto and Schiff said that the most irresponsible course of action would be to continue releasing CFCs until we could actually measure the depletion of the ozone layer. It may have been irresponsible, but that is what the world did.

In the early 1980s, measurements in Antarctica showed what became known as 'the ozone hole'. While the significant depletion of the ozone layer in the southern hemisphere was obviously a health threat to people living in Tasmania, New Zealand and Tierra del Fuego, it did not excite northern hemisphere politicians. However when it subsequently became clear that the thinning of the ozone layer was also posing a risk to north America and western Europe, momentum for change increased rapidly. The relatively timid initial agreement, the Montreal Protocol of 1987, was strengthened at subsequent meetings in Stockholm and then London, where the trenchantly free-market British prime minister Margaret Thatcher supported the unprecedented global intervention, famously saying that we are not owners of the planet 'but tenants with a fully repairing lease'. As I said at the time, although Thatcher was ideologically in favour of allowing free rein to market forces, she had studied chemistry so she understood the science.

The example of the ozone hole shows that it is possible to obtain global agreement to solve an environmental problem. It is also a cautionary tale. The world did not critically depend on CFCs; everything they did, from refrigerator coolants to aerosol propellants, could be done by other compounds and the world now gets on quite well with the substitutes.

By contrast, the fossil fuels that are causing climate change have allowed us to live much more comfortably than previous generations. In principle the damage we are doing to the climate system could be repaired within a few hundred years. If we were to move decisively to reduce our energy use and obtain our supplies from renewable sources like wind and solar, we could stabilise the climate by the end of this century – perhaps during my grand-daughter's lifetime – and then set about restoring it to something like pre-industrial conditions. Sea levels would continue to rise for several hundred years, but most of the damage could be repaired. That future is physically possible, although the political challenges are enormous, especially in the area of energy use.

ENERGY

Australia is an extremely energy-intensive society. The average rate of energy use is now about 6 kilowatts per person, roughly double what it was in 1964. It is equivalent to every Australian driving a small car at about 60 kilometres per hour, 24 hours a day. Of course, we don't drive 24/7 one person to a car. The average reflects the fact that as well as our direct and observable use of energy, when we turn on a light or a gas heater or put fuel into a car, energy is a vital input to every facet of our lives. The food we eat, the water we drink, the buildings we use, our entertainment and the processing of our waste all require large amounts of fuel energy.

Our direct use of energy has also steadily increased over the years. We now have a very high dependence on the private motor vehicle rather than public transport for our travel.

We have steadily increased our use of energy-using appliances, so that the typical home now has a range of devices that did not even exist when I was young. Other tecÿologies have been around for a long time, but the level of use has increased dramatically in recent years. As one example, when I moved to south-east Queensland in 1980, about 5 per cent of dwellings there were air-conditioned. The 2010 figure was 65 per cent! Like everywhere else, Brisbane and its hinterland are being affected by global warming, but not so greatly as to justify that change. It remains true that a well-designed and sensibly oriented building does not need air conditioning. The traditional Queenslander, with its wide verandas and provision for cross-breezes, was a house well suited to the climate, but a brick veneer dwelling is not, especially if it has large windows facing west to catch the afternoon sun. All these changes have significantly increased our average energy use, while the number of us using energy has also been increasing. So overall national electricity demand has more than doubled between 1980 and 2010.

Fossil fuels

The largest fraction of Australian energy use is represented by our electricity consumption and the fuels used to produce that power. Unlike other affluent countries, we still get about 75 per cent of our electricity from coal, the dirtiest of all the fossil fuels. It produces more carbon dioxide per unit energy than oil or gas, and so does more to accelerate climate change. The world was alerted to the possibility that our burning of fossil fuels could be changing the global climate by a 1985 international conference in the Austrian town of Villach. At that time, the scientists were clear that human activity was adding to the concentration of greenhouse gases in the atmosphere and increasing its capacity to trap heat. They were also clear that the average global temperature was increasing, that sea levels were rising and that rainfall patterns were changing, but most cautious scientists were saying that it was too early to be confident that the observed climate change was being caused by human activities of burning fossil fuels and clearing vegetation.

By 1989, I thought the evidence was sufficiently convincing to write *Living in the Greenhouse*, spelling out the scale of the problem and suggesting responses. By 1992, the UN was convinced as well and the Framework Convention on Climate Change was passed at the Rio Earth Summit. Successive conferences of the parties to that convention have attempted to establish a legal framework for slowing climate change. The 1997 meeting established the Kyoto Protocol, which set limits on the production of greenhouse gases by the affluent nations. The Australian government's stance at the Kyoto meeting was a national embarrassment. Our delegation demanded a uniquely generous target, one which effectively allowed us to increase our greenhouse gas production by more than 40 per cent, while other developed countries undertook to reduce theirs.

Given that history, it is outrageous for the Coalition government to be claiming credit for Australia having met our Kyoto obligation; basically it allowed business as usual for us, while it required significant change in Europe and Japan. There was great optimism that the 2009 Copenhagen meeting would negotiate a successor to the Kyoto agreement, but it was only able to put down some broad general principles for the future. The December 2015 meeting in Paris did not produce a legally binding agreement to slow climate change, but it did get global support for a clear statement that the situation is now critical and demands a concerted response.

The International Energy Agency's report *World Energy Outlook 2014* warned that the world is now on track for an increase of about 4 degrees in average global temperature. This is an alarming projection, because the twentieth-century increase in average temperature of less than 1 degree saw rises of about 2.5 degrees in parts of inland Australia. Decisions by China and the USA to curb their domestic production of greenhouse gases provide grounds for cautious optimism that a global solution might still be possible.

Coal also pollutes the local air as it is burned. There is increasing recognition around the world that we need to move away from burning coal. In 2015, the major health journal *The Lancet* published a report estimating the huge benefits to public health that will follow from phasing out coal. It pointed out that the current energy mix results in serious health problems from emission of gaseous pollutants and particulates, from solid wastes, from ionising radiation and the risks of flooding from dams built for hydro-electricity. While hydro is widely recognised as a very clean form of power, it carries significant risks. However, these pale into insignificance compared with the risks from burning coal.

The two main obstacles to phasing out coal are economic and political. In the short term, producing electricity by burning coal in existing power stations is still cheaper than most other technologies, including gas turbines, solar panels and wind turbines. The political obstacle is that the major parties have been strongly associated with the coal industry for many decades, with mining corporations linked to the Liberal Party and donating generously to its funds, while the trade union representing the miners is influential in the ALP. As the evidence has accumulated that global climate change is a very serious threat, thoughtful politicians have seen the need to start moving away from the most carbon-intensive energy forms. There remain significant minorities in right-wing political parties, the US Republicans and the Australian Liberal Party, whose ideological commitment to free enterprise blinds them to the need to move away from coal. In 2015, then prime minister Tony Abbott made the extraordinary statement that 'coal is good for humanity' – and it was repeated in parliament by his dutiful ministers.

The crucial issue for Australia is how we meet our energy needs while also meeting our obligation to play a part in slowing global climate change. Malcolm Turnbull clearly understands the importance of responding to climate change. He was deposed as leader of the parliamentary Liberal Party in 2009, by a group led by Tony Abbott, precisely because he was prepared to adopt a bipartisan approach with the Rudd government to the problem of climate change. Those within the Coalition who are still effectively in denial about the issue appear to have bound the new prime minister Turnbull to continue the Abbott approach of 'masterly inaction'.

Meanwhile, the rest of the world is moving purposefully toward a range of response measures, introducing charges for greenhouse gas production and setting ambitious targets for clean energy production and efficiency improvements. Other countries are astonished that Australia is moving backwards, weakening our renewable energy target and abolishing the modest charge on carbon dioxide production that was introduced while Julia Gillard was prime minister. The policy retreat has slowed the installation of large-scale commercial wind and solar power, but the household revolution is actually gathering pace.

Resources

Australia is not just an energy user, but also a major exporter of fossil fuels. We are so well endowed with minerals that throughout our history we have appeared almost desperate to get rid of them.

Since before the separate colonies came together to make our nation, we have exported our minerals. Throughout the 1990s it seemed as if Australia was genuinely lucky. New mineral resources kept being identified: huge deposits of iron ore in the Pilbara, enormous coal deposits in New South Wales and Queensland, and smaller but significant quantities of other minerals. China's economic development seemed to provide a guaranteed rapidly growing market for whatever minerals we could dig up and ship out. As the new century arrived, China's phenomenal growth continued and new resources such as coal seam gas emerged. The so-called minerals boom provided some employment, partially compensating for the continuing steady decline in manufacturing as cheap imports displaced locally produced goods.

In quantitative terms, coal is our second-largest export earner after iron ore. Successive governments have been almost desperate to see the export coal industry expand, with major public funds being poured into subsidies of ports, rail links and power supplies to encourage new developments. Prime farm land in the Hunter Valley and the Liverpool Plains, important wildlife habitat in the Leard State Forest in New South Wales and the Bimblebox Nature Refuge in Queensland, and even Queensland townships like Acland were seen as expendable when they were in the way of new mines.

The current frenzy of activity probably makes some economic sense in the case of fossil fuels like coal and gas, since they are unlikely to be of any value at all in a few decades' time. Richard Denniss of the Australia Institute has a neat analogy for the coal industry. Imagine an ice-cream van making its way around the suburbs on a hot afternoon, suddenly finding a serious problem: its freezer stops working. The operator would realise that his precious asset for which people are prepared to pay, nice ice-cream, will be a pool of melted mush in a few hours.

ENVIRONMENT

What could he do? He rationally would lower his prices and offer special deals to sell as much of the ice-cream as possible while it was still in a state people were prepared to pay for. The managing director of an export coal company, Denniss argues, is in exactly that position. If they understand climate science, or even if they don't but just observe what is happening in the world market, they will realise that the 'asset' which is the basis of their business – coal which can be burned to produce electricity – will be unsaleable and have no value at all very soon. So they will be desperate to dig it up and get some cash for it while that is still possible.

The proposed huge new coal mines in the Queensland Galilee Basin are already struggling to persuade investors to provide the capital needed, despite the previous state Newman government being prepared to tip large amounts of public money into the project. In 2015, the Australia Institute estimated the annual public subsidy of the mining industry at about $10 billion. The mining industry doesn't appreciate this being described as a subsidy, preferring to portray it as an 'investment' in our future economic development, but critics such as Richard Denniss argue that the funds would be better used developing alternatives to commodity exports.

The coal industry's leaders certainly understand climate change; they even insisted on the coal-loading facility in Newcastle being raised a metre to allow for possible sea level rise during the lifetime of the export terminal. They understand that they will very soon be the proud owners of rocks that nobody will pay good money for, so they are naturally doing what makes commercial sense: trying to lock in purchase agreements that commit their customers for as long as possible.

One expert, Elias Hinckley, has advanced a similar argument for the 2014 decision by Saudi Arabia to increase its oil production.

For several years before that, the Saudis had held back production to keep the world price high, but they suddenly changed their approach and started pumping out more oil, leading to the world price dropping from over US$100 a barrel to about $50. Some observers thought that the Saudis were trying to squeeze out of the market some of the higher-cost producers who had started up as the world price had risen, but Hinckley gave a different explanation. He pointed to climate scientists revealing that most of the known reserves of fossil fuels will have to be left in the ground if the world is to avoid dangerous climate change. That is clearly very bad news for the coal industry, as something like 80 per cent of the known coal has to be left where it is. But it also applies to the oil industry, since we won't be able to use all of the known oil, at least not by burning it and putting carbon dioxide into the air. So one interpretation is that Saudi Arabia has recognised that some of the known oil will not be sold and it is trying to make sure that it sells its oil while that is still possible. As Hinckley put it, 'Global action on carbon dioxide emissions is gaining global acceptance and tecȲological advances are creating foreseeable and viable alternatives to the world's oil dependence. Saudi Arabia has come to the stark realization … that it is a race to produce, regardless of price, so that it will not be leaving its oil in the ground.'

That analysis raises interesting and complex questions about gas exports. One line of thought is that gas is a cleaner fuel than coal or oil, as well as being the easiest energy source to use in place of oil, so its value is likely to increase. That view would suggest that we should be hesitant about selling gas at current prices, since its value is likely to increase. The opposite argument is that gas is also a fossil fuel, albeit the cleanest of them, and so its use also needs to be curtailed to limit the damage we do to the global climate.

ENVIRONMENT

Nuclear power

The other interesting energy question is the continuing debate about nuclear power. In the 1960s, when Horne was writing, there was a widespread view that nuclear power was the energy source of the future. Although Horne did not discuss the nuclear issue, at the time there were several proposals to build nuclear power stations in Australia, but the last of these was scrapped in the early 1970s. Australia had developed a uranium mining industry in the 1950s, essentially to provide the raw material for British nuclear weapons. There is an enduring legacy of degraded land and radioactive waste from those operations at Rum Jungle, Radium Hill and Mary Kathleen, as well as the radioactive debris from the bomb tests. Australian governments under Prime Minister Robert Menzies allowed the UK to explode nuclear weapons in the Monte Bello Islands, off the WA coast, and at Maralinga in South Australia.

In the 1970s, a proposal to develop the Ranger uranium deposit in the Northern Territory led to the Whitlam government establishing an inquiry into its environmental risks. This broadened into a general inquiry into Australia's role in the nuclear industry. Three commissioners, Justice Russell Fox, Professor Charles Kerr and Graeme Kelleher, looked at both the broad issues of the nuclear fuel cycle and the direct environmental consequences of the proposed uranium mine. In terms of the proposed mine, they found the risks could potentially be managed. They noted that the broader debate was confused by assertions that were not backed by evidence, with some opponents of nuclear energy making exaggerated claims about the risks. What surprised them more, the commissioners said, was the lack of objectivity displayed by some supporters, 'including distinguished scientists'. They went on to say that the mining and export of uranium raised two serious issues: the need to manage the radioactive waste produced by nuclear reactors, and the risk that radioactive material would be used to develop nuclear weapons. The report found that the hazards of mining and milling uranium, and those of operating nuclear power stations, did not rule out mining and exporting uranium, provided those activities were properly regulated and controlled. It did, however, add two important qualifications to the proposed expansion of uranium mining and export: it should be subject to safeguards that would assure Australians that the fissile material would not be used to develop nuclear weapons, and we should have been assured that the problem of managing radioactive waste was under control.

While the report had been commissioned by the Whitlam government, the 1975 election brought to power a Coalition government headed by Malcolm Fraser. They did not appear at all concerned about the qualifications and approved the Ranger uranium mine, as well as encouraging other possible developments in the Northern Territory.

In 1977, Fraser calmly stated that the problem of radioactive waste had been solved; I cheekily commented that this was a remarkably modest announcement of a major scientific breakthrough! The ALP, having set up the inquiry, adopted the recommendations and consequently took a policy position opposed to uranium mining and export. That policy was watered down after Bob Hawke became prime minister. A company called Western Mining found a major mineral deposit in northern South Australia at Olympic Dam. While the proposed mine's principal product would be copper, the deposit also contains significant quantities of uranium and gold. The company claimed that the economic viability of the mine would require extracting and exporting uranium as well as copper and gold. Whether this was true or not, the ALP judged that the team led by John Bannon would be unlikely to win the SA state election if they were opposed to the proposed mine. So the ALP national conference adopted the 'three mines policy', which qualified its opposition to the mining and export of uranium by allowing two existing mines and the Olympic Dam proposal. An uncomfortable Hawke admitted under media questioning that it was odd to be opposed in principle to uranium mining but prepared to make an exception for what would be the biggest exporter in the world, but said that it was a pragmatic decision. Western Mining developed the mine and built the town of Roxby Downs to accommodate its workforce. The operation is now part of the portfolio of the international mining company BHP Billiton. Through Ranger and Olympic Dam, Australia is a major exporter of uranium.

While there had been bipartisan support for the principle of not exporting to countries that had not signed the non-proliferation treaty, the Abbott government decided in 2014 to allow uranium to be exported to India. As well as refusing to sign the treaty, India also used Canadian nuclear power technology to develop nuclear weapons, provoking Pakistan to respond and raising the spectre that the hostility between the two neighbours could culminate in nuclear war.

An impossible dilemma

For most of the last 30 years, Australia's role in the nuclear industry has simply been to mine and export uranium. There was a significant change in 2006, when John Howard was prime minister. It was becoming obvious that his inaction on climate change was a political liability, so he set up a task force to explore the possibility of Australia developing nuclear power stations. The group was strongly pro-nuclear, even being headed by the then chair of the board of the Australian Nuclear

Science and Technology Organisation. It toured the world and put together as good a case as it could make for nuclear power in Australia. I reviewed the 2007 report and described the case as distinctly underwhelming. It acknowledged that it would take at least ten years and possibly 15 to build one nuclear power station in Australia. It conceded that nuclear power did not look cost-effective, as it would require both a carbon price and other public support from the government's coffers to make it commercially viable. The report also conceded that radioactive waste management remains an issue of public concern, as does the safety of operating nuclear reactors, but argued that public 'education' could resolve these problems.

The report also showed that nuclear power would not be an effective response to climate change by calculating that a crash program of 25 reactors by 2050 would only reduce the *growth* in Australia's greenhouse gas emissions, not produce the required reduction. It argued that there was a possibility that the economics would look more attractive if Australia were to be a 'late adopter' of a proposed new generation of power reactors that have not yet been built, but I pointed out that this showed an impossible dilemma. For nuclear power to be a timely response to climate change Australia would have to embark immediately on a crash program of building many reactors, but this would not be a cost-effective response. The only hope of it being cost-effective would be to wait for the hypothetical new generation of reactors to be developed and refined, but that would not be a timely response. Either way, nuclear power did not make sense for Australia.

In 2011 the Fukushima accident happened and the support for nuclear power collapsed completely. If the technically sophisticated country of Japan, which had been running nuclear power stations for decades, could not ensure the community would be safe, how could it be responsible to undertake a crash program of reactors in Australia? The Fukushima accident also torpedoed the efforts of the nuclear power industry globally to portray its tecÿology as the low-carbon energy source needed to slow climate change. Proposals for new nuclear power stations have stalled and the uranium market is declining, leading to planned new uranium mining operations and proposed expansions of existing operations being cancelled or deferred. Ironically, the Newman government in Queensland spent large amounts of taxpayers' money in 2014 on a task force that was intended to restart the uranium industry in that state after a 30-year hiatus. That was a complete waste of time and money the government could have used much more constructively.

Desperate times call for desperate measures. The state government of South Australia sees its economic future as problematic. The national Coalition government has withdrawn support for the car industry, leading to decisions by three overseas-owned car manufacturers to announce they will phase out the building of cars in Australia. So thousands of jobs are being lost in Victoria and South Australia. The Abbott government, having promised before the 2014 state election that it would build the next generation of submarines in South Australia, reneged on that commitment after voters re-elected the state ALP government. So South Australia is losing a significant number of jobs in advanced manufacturing, with no obvious replacements. The state governor, Rear Admiral Kevin Scarce, made two speeches in 2014, arguing that the state was missing an opportunity by simply mining and exporting uranium when it could be exploiting other aspects of the nuclear industry such as uranium enrichment, fuel fabrication, waste management or even nuclear power stations. The SA government responded in 2015 by announcing it would set up a royal commission, to be chaired by the now ex-governor, to explore the possible greater involvement of the state in the nuclear industry. A small group at the University of Adelaide has been running the argument that the dry state of South Australia could benefit from nuclear power, providing both relatively low carbon energy and also the power needed to run desalination plants and provide much-needed water. Weird fantasies of becoming the world's radioactive waste repository, or even using radioactive waste in a proposed new generation of nuclear reactors that haven't been designed yet, are being hailed in the local media. One Liberal senator even channelled the delusions of the 1950s when nuclear enthusiasts said its energy would be too cheap to meter. Senator Edwards claimed that nuclear power would not only be so cheap it would be delivered free, but that its adoption would lead to the abolition of several state taxes! The royal commission is due to report in May 2016. Its officers have toured the world to find sources of hope for the nuclear industry. I have been appointed to its expert advisory committee, so I will be involved in trying to ensure that its recommendations are grounded in fact.

Renewables

Some experts now see all fossil fuels being replaced very quickly over the next couple of decades by renewable energy tecŸologies and rapidly improving storage. After I delivered this manuscript to the publisher, I planned an overseas trip which included three days in the UK. I needed a rental car. I found by far the cheapest option was to rent a small electric car, at a price per day about half that of the cheapest petrol or diesel vehicle. That was not the case even a year earlier. The energy scene is changing at a bewildering pace. Respected economic analyst Paul Gilding has argued that we are already seeing the inexorable slide of the fossil fuel industry toward its inevitable end. In 2015, journalist

ENVIRONMENT

Joy Rogers reported that the US price of solar electricity was below 4 cents a kilowatt-hour. This is not only far less than we pay in Australia for our power; it is comparable with the cost of generating electricity from fossil fuels. So there is no longer even an economic case for preferring coal to wind and solar. Just as the Organization of Petroleum Exporting Countries' (OPEC) long-time spokesman Sheik Yamani observed, the Stone Age did not end because we ran out of stones and the Oil Age will not end because we run out of oil. Just as stones were replaced by more flexible materials, fossil fuels are now being supplanted by cleaner and more flexible energy technologies. The move away from fossil fuels will improve our privileged position in facing the future. The only physical resource Australia imports in significant quantities is oil. So the end of the Oil Age is also the end of the age in which we need to import resources.

In terms of renewable resources, we are outrageously blessed. One figure sums this up: the amount of solar energy that hits the Australian landmass in one summer day is about half the total annual energy use for the entire world! All 7 billion people in a year only use about twice as much energy as the sun delivers to us in a day. Put another way, on a summer day an area about 7 kilometres square receives as much energy as our total installed electrical capacity. With the average conversion efficiency of modern solar cells being about 16 per cent, we would only need an area about 17 kilometres square to provide as much power as the entire national electricity system. Of course, the sun doesn't shine at night, so solar energy has to be supplemented by other systems. At the moment, by far the most cost-effective is wind power. While the Coalition government has been doing its best to sabotage renewable energy, ordinary Australians have been voting with their roofs. Despite little encouragement from governments, about 1.5 million homes now have solar cells on their roof, and a further half million or so have solar hot water. Large-scale wind power has been installed on some of the most cost-effective sites in the southern states. In 2014, South Australia got about 40 per cent of all its electricity from wind and solar; the apex was reached on 30 September that year, when all the power used in the entire working day came from solar and wind, with absolutely no contribution at all from fossil fuels.

The group Beyond Zero Emissions released a report in 2010, showing that it is entirely possible to produce all of our power needs from a mix of renewable energy tecÿologies. More recently, a group at the University of New South Wales used the data from the so-called National Energy Market, which covers the eastern states and South Australia, to determine the capacity of renewables to meet our needs. Ben Elliston, Iain MacGill and Mark Diesendorf took the hour-by-hour figures for an entire year to show that the demand can be satisfied by a combination of solar, wind and a small amount of energy from biomass, together with the existing hydro-electric schemes. That exercise showed the total cost of meeting all our estimated energy needs from now to 2050 from renewables is virtually the same as that of assuming we continue to use the present approach, with about 75 per cent of the energy coming from coal. Continuing that approach would require not just replacing the old coal-fired power stations as they reach the end of their useful lives, but also mining and transporting over 100 million tonnes of coal a year. In 2015, old coal-fired power stations were being closed down at Port Augusta in South Australia and Anglesea in Victoria, partly because of falling demand and partly because of increasing supply from wind and solar.

A new study of electricity cost in Australia was released by Bloomberg New Energy Finance in July 2015. It concluded that the costs of power from new installations in Australia would now be $74 per megawatt-hour for a wind farm, $92 for a base-load gas installation, $105 for a large-scale solar cell array and $119 for a new coal-fired power station. The Australian head of the organisation was quoted as saying: 'Wind is already the cheapest, and solar photovoltaic panels will be cheaper than gas in around two years, in 2017'. His projection is that costs of wind and solar will both continue to decline, but solar will fall faster and 'will become the dominant source'. So there is already a strong economic case for an approach of phasing out the old coal-fired power stations and replacing them with renewables.

There is no doubt that a mix of renewables can meet all our needs. It will require significant capital investment in the next decade to provide the generating capacity. After that, with no fuel needed, the only cost of delivering energy is the interest bill on the capital, plus a minuscule maintenance budget. It won't be 'power too cheap to meter', as was once claimed for nuclear energy, but it will be clean energy that isn't changing the global climate.

It will also allow the transport system to be converted from petroleum fuels, with their serious legacy of polluted air and consequent large-scale respiratory distress for the urban population, to electric vehicles. That raises the issue of storage. I used to show my students a clipping saying that the electric car was clearly the car of the future as it is clean, quiet, efficient and non-polluting. All that was required for it to take over, the article said, was an advance on storage beyond the lead-acid battery, predicting that advance to be 'just around the corner'. It was written in 1903! Sadly, over a hundred years later, we were still waiting for that advance – but now it finally seems to have arrived. In 2015, the US-based Tesla Corporation announced a huge investment of $5 billion in a factory to mass-produce their new batteries and achieve economies of scale that will drive down prices. Where the cost of a battery pack to power an electric car has traditionally been about $25,000, making the vehicle a real luxury item, industry experts are predicting it will be about $5,000 by 2020. With an electric motor cheaper to build than a petrol or diesel engine, we could see a very rapid transition, particularly for urban motoring. The use of electric cars for inter-urban trips is a bigger challenge, but not an insuperable one. A modern electric car will travel about 200 kilometres on one charge of its battery pack. A 'super-charging station' will fully charge an electric car's battery pack in less than half an hour, a reasonable time for a driver to have a coffee and recharge their personal batteries to continue the drive. There is already an extensive chain of these charging stations along major arterial roads in England. In 2015, it was announced that one would be built at Goulburn, roughly halfway between Sydney and Canberra, to make sure that electric cars would be able to make that drive. If it is successful, we could well see the same happen here as in the UK, a rapid rollout of support to allow electric cars to make long journeys as well as short suburban trips.

The renewable resource which could be a limiting factor for Australia is water. We are the driest inhabited continent and also the continent with the most variable rainfall, so harvesting and efficiently using our water is a critical issue, especially for food production. Climate change is already affecting water supply to the Perth region, while Adelaide's dependence on water from the Murray River means that it also faces future problems. But far more water is used for agriculture than as urban water supplies, so food production is a critical issue, and one which raises the problem of whether economic growth has natural limits.

LIMITS TO GROWTH

The Club of Rome

Our leaders, in common with others around the world, continue to deny the inconvenient truth spelled out by the first report to global think-tank the Club of Rome more than 40 years ago: there are limits to growth. Titled *The Limits to Growth: A Report for the Club of Rome's Project on the Predicament of Mankind*, it caused a storm by using the computer models which had just become available to show that the projected future growth of human society would lead to serious problems. The report concluded that if the 1970s trends of growth in population, resource use, industrial production, agricultural output and pollution were all to continue, the world would reach limits to growth within a hundred years, with the most likely result 'a rather sudden and uncontrollable decline in both population and industrial capacity' – in other words – economic, social and environmental collapse in the early to middle decades of this century, well within the projected hundred years. The cover of my battered early paperback edition of the book says 'even under the most optimistic assumptions about advances in technology, the world cannot support present rates of economic and population growth for more than a few decades'.

Importantly, the report did not predict that this collapse would happen; it projected that outcome as one possibility, if the existing trends were to continue. It also said that it was entirely possible to redirect human development onto a path that would be sustainable into the distant future and that offered the prospect of a desirable future, one in which all humans would have their basic needs met and be able to realise their full potential. The report's conclusion was that political decisions would determine which future would eventuate.

The sceptics

In an ideal world, leaders might have been expected to embrace the report, grateful to have been shown the way to avoid serious problems. Instead, it was demonised by people who found its very title *The Limits to Growth* an affront, those who deeply believe that our world has no limits. They blatantly misrepresented its message, claimed that the report simplistically stated we would run out of resources by 1990 or suffocate in our own wastes by the year 2000, then triumphantly said that 'the Club of Rome got it wrong'; one arrogant British economist, Professor Wilfred Beckerman, even posed the question, 'How stupid do you have to be to join this club?' The critics usually appealed to readers to have faith in our ability to avoid the projected problems. This approach was famously described by economist Alan Coddington as 'cheer-mongering' – portray the problem in simple terms, make the obvious observation that the real world is more complicated than that simplistic version, then express a cheerful optimism that our tecŸical ingenuity or the power of market forces will enable us to resolve the complex situation in agreeable ways. It works, Coddington argues, because it tells people what they want to hear: don't listen to the alarmists who will tell you about problems, human ingenuity and the market have made us more comfortable now than we were 50 years ago, so you can be confident that things will be better still in another 50 years.

The Lomborg effect

A recent example of this approach is the phenomenon of Danish statistician Bjorn Lomborg. He rose from the obscurity of teaching statistics to politics students at a small Danish university when he published a book called *The Skeptical Environmentalist*. In fact, it contained nothing of the proud scientific tradition of scepticism, of demanding evidence for assertions, of keeping an open mind and suspending belief until the data becomes available. The book was a shameless exercise in cherry-picking data and quoting quite reputable scientists out of context to give the appearance of solid evidence for the author's belief that all the world's major environmental problems are exaggerated. Although the exercise had no scientific credibility, Lomborg was hailed by business interests because he was saying what they wanted to hear, that environmental problems could safely be ignored while they got on with their primary task of making money. Briefly funded by a right-wing government in Denmark, he was then supported by US financial interests when the Danish government changed. This money allowed him to hold what he called 'consensus conferences' in which he brought together economists to talk about priorities for development. Not surprisingly, the economists agreed that the environmental problems were not urgent and the top priority should be encouraging economic growth, promoting the delusion that people in the poorest countries could aspire to live in the material comfort now associated with wealthier areas.

This specific incident is a reminder of a general truth. Most economists argue that economic growth has been the key to improving material living standards in the historic past, so the only hope of lifting the world's poor out of their desperate living conditions is further growth. The implication is that continuing growth will eventually allow the poorest people in the world to live a life of middle-class comfort. Those making that claim usually ignore the scale of resource use and the consequent waste production that would be needed in that future utopian world. Any critics who question the claim are accused of heartless disregard for the conditions of the poor nations. Even the export of coal, a shameless exercise in trying to make money before the world agrees that the fossil fuels should be left in the ground, has been portrayed by Coalition government ministers as our duty to lift the world's poorest out of 'energy poverty'. It is a dishonest claim on three levels. First, the poorest people would not be able to afford coal-fired electricity even if it were offered to them. Second, countries like India and Pakistan are investing heavily in local solar power, the most promising way out of 'energy poverty' for poor rural areas. Third, the poorest will suffer disproportionately from the accelerating climate change caused by burning the coal.

The issue of trusting economic growth to solve the problems of poverty and climate change became a political topic in 2015. The Abbott government decided to bypass the normal peer-review methods for funding research and allocate $4 million to the University of Western Australia to set up a Consensus Centre, to be headed by Lomborg. Academics at the university were outraged when they heard what the university managers had agreed to do. The outcry led the vice-chancellor to back down and announce that the university would not go ahead with the proposal. Undeterred by this setback, the Coalition government started shopping around to try to find another university that would be prepared to set aside normal academic standards for the sake of $4 million of public money. The intention of the exercise was obvious: to have an allegedly independent centre telling the government what it wants to hear, that environmental issues and inequality are unimportant and the limited aid budget should be directed to stimulating economic growth. No university was prepared to abandon its academic standards and accept the $4 million on offer to host the proposed centre, so the offer was quietly withdrawn.

The science

While the rhetoric of business leaders and politicians suggests that all of the world's problems can be solved by further growth, the science paints a realistic and much more depressing picture. Recent analysis of the global situation by CSIRO's Dr Graham Turner has shown that all the growth trends identified in *The Limits to Growth* over 40 years ago have indeed continued, putting the world right on target for the grim future of collapse. I attended the 2013 Fenner Conference and chaired its final session, which reviewed all the evidence and came to a similar conclusion. The conference proceedings have been published as a book, *Sustainable Futures: Linking Population, Resources and the Environment*, edited by Jenny Goldie and Katharine Betts. It sounds a clear warning about the need to take a different approach.

Jörg Friedrichs's 2014 book *The Future Is Not What It Used to Be: Climate Change and Energy Scarcity* is an important challenge to conventional thinking. He notes that several past civilisations have been seriously affected by energy scarcity, even in the last hundred years. Japan's energy shortage in the first half of the twentieth century led to its attempt to obtain resources by military action in the 1940s. Cuba and North Korea both had critical problems producing food after the 1989 collapse of the Soviet Union restricted their access to oil; food shortages are still a problem in North Korea. Earlier societies have been impacted by climate change. As an extreme example, the Vikings settled in Iceland and Greenland during the medieval warm period about 1,000 years ago when Greenland was indeed a green land rather than an icy waste. Both of the settlements were then endangered about 500 years later by the so-called Little Ice Age in western Europe, when the Thames froze solidly enough for Londoners to hold frost fairs and roast whole bullocks on the ice.

The Greenland settlement, unable to produce food in the colder climate, collapsed. In an historical example with an important lesson for us all, the people in Iceland survived by adapting, turning to fishing to obtain from the sea the protein they were unable to produce on land. They also started trading dried fish for the fruit and vegetables they could no longer grow. The moral is that being willing to adapt is critical when faced with climate change, as we all are now.

Friedrichs argues that industrial societies as a whole face the twin threats of declining oil production and global climate change. A US oil expert, M King Hubbert, originally developed the concept of 'peak oil'. He analysed in 1956 the pattern of US oil discoveries and subsequent production, concluding that US domestic oil production would peak in about 1971 and lead to the USA becoming a significant purchaser on the world market. Hubbert speculated that this could change the balance of the oil market between producers and consumers. He was right. US oil production did peak in 1971, leading to increasing US imports. The body representing the oil-producing nations, the Organization of Petroleum Exporting Countries (OPEC), realised that it had the opportunity to demand higher prices. At the time, the price of crude oil on the world market was about US$1.90 a barrel. OPEC made what was seen as an outrageous demand: that the consuming nations should pay $5 a barrel. The purchasers resisted, so OPEC halted production. There was a fuel crisis in the northern hemisphere. I was working in the UK at the time and supplies dried up. I read reports of fist-fights at bowsers as service stations ran out of petrol. In the more violent culture of the USA, gunfights were reported as motorists argued about the dwindling supplies. Eventually it was accepted that OPEC had to be paid the price it was asking. Having established that it had the whip hand, the organisation increased its demands. This led to an unprecedented inflation of oil prices, from below US$2 per barrel in 1972 to nearly $30 in 1979. Since Hubbert's prediction had proved correct, several analysts considered the available data about global oil supplies and predicted, as far back as the mid-1970s, that world production of conventional oil would peak in about 2010. It did. Since then, oil production has been supplemented by extraction from deep water, from polar regions and from gas condensates – in all cases at increasing cost and increasing environmental impacts. The 2010 BP oil spill in the Gulf of Mexico was a dramatic reminder of the risks of extracting oil from deep ocean water.

The two threats mentioned by Friedrichs are intertwined because almost all the possible supplements to declining production of conventional oil involve greater contributions to climate change. At the time of writing, there was a concerted shift toward more carbon-intensive oil production, extending to 'unconventional' sources such as tar sands and oil shales. That approach certainly accelerates climate change. Friedrichs cites economists and politicians who are in denial about these serious issues, but they cannot escape the inevitable logic: growth in both population and per capita resource use cannot continue forever on a finite planet. There are legitimate disagreements about whether we have already reached what Friedrichs calls 'choke points', but he makes a solid case that these problems are now serious threats to our future. His prognosis is not cheerful. After reviewing the response of early societies to the sort of problems we now face, he concludes that the level of complexity of industrial societies makes it 'increasingly hard to envisage progressive and complex solutions'. He argues that it is also difficult to imagine a voluntary return to 'a lower level of social and political complexity' which might be sustainable. This leads him to a gloomy conclusion that the most likely outcome is 'a long emergency', posing the real possibility that some modern states might respond as Japan did in 1941, attempting to meet their needs by military force.

Another recent book by an Australian author makes a similar but broader argument. Kerryn Higgs's book *Collision Course: Endless Growth on a Finite Planet* argues that the industrial system is on a 'collision course' with the capacity of natural systems to provide our needs and manage our waste products. The book tackles head-on the argument that continuing economic growth will solve the problems of the world's poorest. Higgs shows that the neoliberal economic agenda has not benefited the poor but widened inequality within and between nations. As well as quoting Dr Graham Turner's analysis, mentioned above, she draws on the work of systems ecologists Charles Hall and JoŸ Day, who also conclude that further growth is problematic beyond a relatively short time horizon. As Higgs says, the overall pie has been enlarged by the dramatic economic growth of the last 50 years, but its growth has 'utterly failed to yield sufficiently large slices to afford everyone even modest security'. The resulting increased prosperity is, she says, 'concentrated among a privileged minority', while more than half the world's people remain desperately poor. Higgs argues that the pursuit of economic growth, which has historically benefited most of us in this country, is now a serious threat to our future. Higgs reinforces the obvious conclusion that climate change is the most obvious and immediate threat, as is now recognised globally. According to a 2015 survey of more than 45,000 people in 40 countries by the US-based Pew Research Center, designed to measure perceptions of international threats, climate change is viewed as the 'top concern' by people around the world. People in 19 of the 40 nations surveyed cite climate change as their biggest worry, making it the most widespread concern of any issue in the survey – a greater threat than terrorism.

Dr Michael Dorsey, a member of the Club of Rome and interim director of energy and environment at the Joint Center for Political and Economic Studies, recently sounded a clear warning about the need to respond to increasing public concern by rethinking regulatory approaches. He said, 'If we accept the fact that carbon pollution drives both human mortality and morbidity, compromises ecosystems, and threatens society, then institutions and firms that produce carbon pollution, as well as those who opt to finance carbon polluters, are akin to those who work with entities engaged in and financing terrorism.' Dorsey went on to note that some elected officials have proposed using laws designed to fight organised crime against those who deny the unfolding climate crisis. Patricia Lerner of Greenpeace International said that it is not surprising that nearly half of the nations surveyed cited climate change as their biggest worry. 'It's those on the front lines of climate change, and its catastrophic results, who are often the first to recognise the real threat it presents,' she said. Lerner attacked 'the myopia of governments and businesses which are failing to recognise climate change is an issue that threatens all of us – wherever we live', singling out for special mention 'the deadly cycle of drilling in the Arctic for oil which is burned, creating CO_2, which then further melts the Arctic'.

Climate change is certainly not the only indicator of the increasing stress put on natural systems by increasing human demands. It might not even be the most serious problem. But it will have serious impacts on people living in low-lying areas around the Asia–Pacific region. All of these environmental considerations will have an impact on how we think about our place in the world.

GEOGRAPHY

Among people who take a sophisticated interest in Asia it is fairly common ground that the term is too wide in reference for any except an arbitrary geographical meaning ... there is in reality a whole lot of different countries with different histories and different cultures.
—The Lucky Country, fifth edition, p. 109

Donald Horne suggested that it is perhaps because of our origins as a British colonial dumping ground that Australia has rarely paid close attention to its position on the map. This has resulted in our leaders treating Asia simplistically and ignorantly as a homogenous landmass that can be a valuable economic trading partner but has nothing to offer in cultural or political terms. Similarly, Australians have preferred to ignore our history of dispossessing Indigenous Australians, and the cultural and psychological legacies of those actions. When it comes to foreign policy and defence, we have moved from a British-centric view to blindly following the USA in its global strategies of economic and military dominance. We produce more than enough food to feed our population but use unsustainable farming practices that do not account for our unique environment. We continue to ignore the impacts of climate change on the Pacific island states.

IGNORING ASIA

In 1964, Horne observed that our leaders were mostly still in denial of our geographical reality or offering oversimplified generalisations about Asia, in a way they never would about continents like Europe. All but the most uneducated of our politicians recognise that there are profound historical, social and cultural differences between France and Germany, between

Italy and Spain, between England and Ireland, but few show even that level of basic understanding about the complex diversity of the region to the north and west of Australia. As Horne said in the 1998 preface to the fifth edition of his book, one of our prime ministers 'acted as if he alone had discovered Asia' while another baldly told a Jakarta state banquet that 'Australia is not part of Asia'.

Education

When Horne wrote his book, our education system had little emphasis on learning any of the major Asian languages or about the history of China, India, Japan or Indonesia. School history was mainly British with a romanticised account of the British exploration and colonisation of this country. Any reference to Asia centred on former British colonies like India, or the remaining colonial legacies like Hong Kong. If young Australians studied a foreign language, it was usually French. If they took a second language, it was either Latin or German. In that sense, we had adopted the British model of schooling when we were part of that empire. Like Donald Horne, I enjoyed an afternoon off school in the 1950s when we celebrated Empire Day on 24 May, chosen because it had been the birthday of Queen Victoria! Then the word 'empire' became embarrassing and was re-badged as the 'British Commonwealth of Nations', but the education did not change. Nor did our overall orientation. My first passport, issued after *The Lucky Country* was published, identified me as an Australian citizen and British subject – a designation which immigration officials found amusing when I passed through some Asian countries in 1967, as I mentioned earlier.

Not until the 1970s did a few schools start to offer one or more of the principal Asian languages. The numbers studying

French, German and Latin had been inflated by the matriculation requirements of some universities in general and some courses – usually medicine, law and pharmacy. When those provisions were withdrawn about a decade after Horne wrote his book, the percentage of final-year school students studying a language other than English collapsed from being a majority to not much more than 10 per cent. The increasing cultural diversity of Australia since then has brought with it a pressure for 'community languages', those spoken by significant numbers of Australians, to be taught in schools.

Since 1964 there has been a very noteworthy change in the pattern of second-language study in Australia. In the latest figures I could find, in a 2009 report quoting 2006 data, the most common languages studied in our schools were Japanese and Italian, each with over 300,000 students, followed by Indonesian and French, each with just over 200,000 students. German was next, with about 125,000 students, followed by Chinese with about 80,000. The only other languages studied by more than 10,000 students were (in descending order from about 25,000) Arabic, Spanish, Greek and Vietnamese. This is the most generous picture, including those programs in which students do only 100 hours of study of the language chosen. Although over 130 languages are taught somewhere in the Australian school system, including about 50 Indigenous languages, the numbers for most programs are very small. The fact that Japanese competes with Italian for the highest numbers, with French and Indonesian almost equal behind them and German next, shows that the language teaching in Australian schools is about evenly balanced between our European past and our Asian future. It is also obvious from Year 12 figures that most of the study of Asian languages is only in the earlier years of schooling. Education leaders decided in 2009 to try to improve the situation and set an aspirational target that by 2020, 12 per cent of students completing secondary school would be studying an Asian language in Year 12. At that time the enrolments were about half that level: about 5,000 studying Chinese, about 4,000 taking Japanese, 1,300 Indonesian and fewer than 200 Korean.

Historical distrust

Horne made the point in 1964 that the concept of 'Asian' had made sense only as an antithesis of 'European'. The European domination of Asia ended during and after World War II with the retreat of the British from India, Malaya and Singapore, the retreat of the Dutch from New Guinea and the archipelago that became Indonesia, the retreat of the French from Vietnam and Cambodia, and the retreat of the Portuguese from Goa. The result is, as Horne put it, 'a collection of sub-continents, themselves divided'. He observed that the differences between, and in some cases within, Asian nations are huge. Japanese tend to look down on their neighbours, especially Koreans. Overseas Chinese communities tend to see themselves, Horne said, as 'inheritors of the Central Kingdom, the true governors of Asia'. He continued, 'Everyone who is not Chinese or Indian distrusts both the Chinese and the Indians. Among the Chinese and Indians themselves there are differences of race and class.' Not only are physical differences between different groups in Asia greater than between different Europeans, Horne argued, but there are greater differences between stages of economic development, greater disparities between rich and poor, and much greater religious and cultural diversity. 'While there is some sense of a common civilisation in Europe,' Horne concluded, 'there is none in Asia – except perhaps among those top people who are Westernised.'

Horne argued that the notion of 'Asia' as a homogenous and threatening entity was a product of history. Distrust of the Chinese had been a continuing social problem in the goldfields of the nineteenth century, with outbreaks of violence in New South Wales and Victoria. The first law passed by the new Commonwealth parliament after federation in 1901 was to prohibit Asian migrant workers. World War II and the threat of Japanese invasion was followed by the rise of communism in China. This in turn led to Australian governments supporting anti-communist military campaigns by the British in Malaya and the USA in Korea and Vietnam. These conflicts reinforced a perception that the small population of Australia, at that time overwhelmingly of British descent, risked being swamped by a tsunami of Asians sweeping south. 'We must populate our empty north or it will be over-run by the Asian hordes' was a common aphorism and the phrase 'the yellow peril' was still used by politicians. I remember the broadcaster Cyril Pearl making the obvious point that Java was densely populated and Arnhem Land had very few people for many thousands of years before the British invaded Australia. The reason, he pointed out, is that Java has rich deep volcanic soils that allow it to support a large population, while Arnhem Land has old nutrient-poor soil that is not suited to agriculture. Saying that our empty north would be invaded if we didn't populate it, Pearl said, was like Algerians worrying about the Sahara Desert being over-run if they didn't farm it.

Underlying the discourse, as Horne pointed out, was an openly racist distrust of non-Europeans. The official migration policy of Australia was informally known as the 'White Australia policy'. The formal rules allowed the government to require any intended migrant to take a dictation test in any European language; the test was obviously designed to exclude anyone the government did not want to enter the country. One report says that nobody passed the test after 1909; Gaelic was famously chosen in 1934 to exclude the Czech political activist Egon Kisch. Until the provision was removed by the passing of the *Migration Act* in 1958, our immigration policy assumed that no level of fluency in any Asian language was sufficient to pass the test; intending migrants had to demonstrate fluency in a *European* tongue. Only a few years before writing his book, Horne had caused a storm when he became editor of *The Bulletin* magazine and removed from its front cover the slogan 'Australia for the White Man'. This precipitated what Horne called 'pathological abuse'. A significant fraction of the magazine's subscribers immediately cancelled their subscriptions in protest at the step back from *The Bulletin*'s traditional ethos! In fact, that slogan was a shortened version of *The Bulletin*'s original motto, which had included a racist reference to Chinese people.

Narrow economic engagement

Australia has seen Asian countries, as Horne observed 50 years ago, through a narrow economic prism: 'little more than an economic machine out of which we can make a buck'. Our engagement with Asian countries is still largely at the economic level, selling raw materials to them and buying their finished products. Horne wrote that the Australia into which he was born was 'a rather stupid place' that covered 'its imports bill by exporting unprocessed commodities' with 'a philistine rhetoric that concealed, for instance, how the success of the export industries … depended partly on research scientists who were among the best in the world'. This is a very significant point. Australia was successfully exporting minerals and agricultural produce as a consequence of the investment in research that began in the 1930s with the precursor of CSIRO. In 1964, it was still oriented mainly toward science that helped primary production, especially agriculture. Our only rural university at that time, University of New England, also did research to help farmers and graziers. This research was accurately seen as a collective investment in our economic future.

The change in the pattern of Australian trade since Horne wrote his book has been a move away from Europe, especially the UK, toward Asia, especially Japan and China. I remember the shock and sense of betrayal in the 1960s when the UK first canvassed the possibility of joining the European 'Common Market', cutting off the most obvious outlet for our primary produce like meat and butter. With the UK's subsequent formal move into the European Union, Australian producers were forced to look for export opportunities in our region. The overall emphasis of our trade, however, remains very much as Horne described it. If anything, his observation is more obviously true today. In 1964 Australia produced radios and television sets, electronic equipment for communications and navigation, cars and larger transport vehicles, boats and light aircraft. Over the last 50 years, we have systematically run down our manufacturing capacity. The last large-scale vehicle building plants will close in the next few years. Appliances and electronic equipment in our stores mostly come from overseas. We even import such basic products as clothes and shoes. Our escalating import bill for advanced manufactures has been covered by exporting ever-increasing quantities of unprocessed raw materials, principally iron ore and coal. The only change is that the exports now are much more likely to go to China, Japan or Korea than the UK or other European countries; equally, the imports of labour-intensive goods like textiles, clothing and footwear are now predominantly from China, while the imports of knowledge-intensive products like cars or computers are mostly from Japan or Korea. Every now and again there is a call for processing of our minerals to add value, but few of these schemes come to fruition – and when they do, as in smelting of bauxite to produce aluminium, the economics of processing in Australia is so unattractive that the industry survives only with massive public subsidies. In that specific case of aluminium, the Australia Institute calculated that the subsidy is so large and the number of people employed so small that it would save taxpayers money if the industry closed down and every worker was given $100,000 a year to go fishing! The broader issue has been a bone of contention for decades. Over thirty years ago, in his famous book *Sleepers, Wake! Tecÿology and the Future of Work,* Barry Jones, who became Minister for Science in the Hawke government, lamented the fact that we exported iron ore at $50 a tonne and bought it back as processed steel products like ball bearings at more like $5,000 a tonne. The failure to add value to commodities before exporting them, a cause of concern to Donald Horne, remains an issue today.

More generally, the entire economic model of exporting large volumes of low-value commodities to pay for our imports can only work, even in principle, while long-distance freight transport is powered by cheap petroleum fuels and countries like China continue to buy our cheap commodities. Most decision-makers can't see a problem with this approach. I heard a senior government official in the 1980s, David Buckingham, praise the way the market 'turns our coal and iron ore into cars and computers'. Our leaders still obsess about the possibility of 'free trade agreements', in the hope of selling more cheap commodities to countries like China. To reinforce this point, government sources hailed a recently negotiated trade agreement with China as enabling the export of large amounts of milk, expecting the community to see this as a desirable investment in our economic future. Of course, in the short term it may benefit a few dairy farmers, but that industry has already been run down significantly. Many of the remaining dairies are owned by foreign interests, so we may well see Chinese companies exporting milk to China. Competing with New Zealand to export milk products to countries such as China could very well drive prices down further.

FOREIGN POLICY AND DEFENCE

At the end of World War II, Europe was divided at peace talks in Yalta, leading to the Soviet Union (based on Russia) controlling eastern Europe: the Baltic countries of Latvia, Lithuania and Estonia as well as Hungary, Poland, Czechoslovakia, Yugoslavia and Albania, with Germany divided into East Germany, controlled by the Soviet Union, and West Germany, effectively controlled by the USA. British prime minister Winston Churchill famously said 'an iron curtain' had descended across the middle of Europe, locking the eastern countries into what was essentially a Russian empire. Australian foreign policy was dominated by recognition that the intervention of the USA in the Pacific war had saved Australia from being invaded by Japan. In 1949, the communists led by Mao Tse Tung overthrew the Chinese Kuomintang government under Chiang Kai-shek, who retreated to Taiwan and set up what purported to be an alternative government of China on that island. For decades, the USA and Australia refused to recognise the communist regime in Beijing, calling it 'Red China' and supporting the fiction that the Taiwanese group was still the legal government.

Critics have suggested that we moved smoothly from being a British colony to being a US colony, as our elected leaders slavishly followed the lead of Washington. When a civil war broke out in Korea in the early 1950s between communists and right-wing forces, China supported the communists based in the north of the country, so we joined the USA in sending troops to support the southern army. The war became bogged down in a stalemate, leading to the country being divided along the 38th parallel of latitude into the two halves that continue to this day, the pro-US south and the pro-China north.

Also in the mid-1950s, Vietnamese rebels pushed the French colonial power out of their country, but the USA was alarmed by the leftist views of the new government. They supported the establishment of a puppet regime in the southern city of Saigon, leading inevitably to a civil war. The USA first sent 'advisers' to help the southern group, then started sending troops and urged Australia and New Zealand to join them. What is known in Vietnam as the American War was a long and dirty affair, lasting more than a decade and costing hundreds of thousands of lives, mostly Vietnamese. At the height of the conflict, close to a million foreign troops were in Vietnam, trying to prop up the pro-US regime. Supporting the war was a contentious issue in Australia. Essentially the Liberal Party and its coalition partners supported the military action, while the ALP did not. It was hard to persuade young men to volunteer to fight in Vietnam, so the Coalition government brought in conscription, choosing by ballot which 20-year-olds would be forced to join the military. This was a divisive move, as at the time the voting age was 21, so those being drafted for military service could not show their displeasure at the ballot box. Supporting the US military in Vietnam was driven by a naïve geopolitical view of the world. The Liberal Party and its supporters espoused what they called 'the domino theory' – the belief that communism would inevitably spread south, country by country, if not forcibly arrested in Vietnam. I remember a NSW politician saying 'Better in Bien Hoa than in Beardy Street', encapsulating his view that the southward march of communism had to be halted in Vietnam or it would inevitably flow all the way down the Australian mainland to the centre of the peaceful country town of Armidale. The theory was spectacularly ill-informed, ignoring both the strong nationalist flavour of the Vietnamese government and their centuries-old hostility toward their northern neighbour, China.

It is now history that the US attempt to impose its will on Vietnam failed. The war effectively ended in 1975 with the fall of Saigon, which was renamed Ho Chi Minh City after the Vietnamese leader during the war years. The significant flow-on effect for Australia was that large numbers of Vietnamese people who had supported the US military action fled the country, becoming the first wave of 'boat people' to seek refuge in Australia. The Liberal Party was seriously conflicted between its traditional anti-Asian migration policy and recognition of its responsibility for the plight of the refugees. The Fraser government allowed large numbers of Vietnamese to enter Australia. Those immigrants were inevitably inclined to a right-wing political stance, so arguably the Liberal Party stood to benefit by allowing them to become Australian citizens. Vietnam remains an independent nation and an increasingly popular holiday destination, but Australia has an enduring legacy of the conflict. While those who fought in the two world wars did so with the almost universal support of the country, those who fought in Vietnam did not. A significant minority of Australians thought the exercise was ill-advised. So the returning veterans faced social tension to compound what we now recognise as post-traumatic stress. Many of them, and their families, remain casualties of their experience to this day.

As if to demonstrate that they have learned nothing from the earlier experiences, many of our recent politicians have adopted the same slavish alignment with whatever ill-judged military adventure the US government begins. In the 1980s they armed the Taliban to fight against Russians in Afghanistan, then realised they had installed a militantly Islamic regime and began arming local warlords to fight against the Taliban; we joined in the fight, although it is almost impossible to argue that the colour of the government in Kabul has strategic importance for Australia. George W Bush's regime decided to respond to the 2001 Al Qa'ida attack on the World Trade Center by attacking Iraq, justifying it with the ludicrous and dishonest claim that Saddam Hussein possessed 'weapons of mass destruction'. Despite the biggest public protests in Australian history, the Howard government repeated the claim and sent troops to Iraq, again ignoring the obvious consequences.

There is now a solid view among informed analysts like Seumas Milne and Dilly Hussain that the rise of ISIS or Daesh is a direct result of the ill-judged military intervention in Iraq and the consequent destabilisation of that country. The US military actions in Afghanistan and Iraq are direct consequences of their earlier armed interventions in those countries. In 2015, then prime minister Tony Abbott, who was a minister in the Howard government and so involved in the disastrous invasion of Iraq and the problematic intervention in Afghanistan, was frantically aligning his government with the latest US actions in the Middle East. At one level, it was easy to infer that he was ignorant of the consequences. Some observers suggested another motive: that he may have hoped his actions would provoke Australian Muslims to react with terrorist activity, since that would appear to justify his policies. Whether that is true or not, Malcolm Turnbull as prime minister has certainly adopted more inclusive language than Abbott's constant repetition of the slogans of 'Team Australia' and the 'death cult' of ISIS. Whether it was intended or not, there can be no doubt that the following of US military adventures has made Australia a less stable and less safe country. We are now widely seen as an American client state, rather than an independent nation. Being seen as hostile to Islam is not just making Australia less stable internally by alienating young Muslims, it is also affecting our relationship with our nearest neighbour, as Indonesia is the world's most populous Muslim nation.

That inevitably flows on to our defence posture being inseparably aligned to defending US interests. In 2015, Australian military forces were engaging in joint exercises with Americans, as if preparing to wage war together. Successive Australian governments have allowed US agencies to set up spy bases on our soil, sometimes describing them as 'joint facilities', but there is little evidence that we have any control over the activities. With growing tension between the USA and China, our most important trading partner, it seems short-sighted to throw away the opportunity to act as an honest broker between the two superpowers. Respected defence analysts like Hugh White of the Australian National University (ANU) have argued that we should take a more independent stance, especially as US interests do not necessarily align with ours. The issue is no longer political. While the ALP took an independent stance when the USA was attacking Vietnam in the 1960s, since Bob Hawke became its leader in 1983 the party has been aligned with the USA as strongly as the Coalition. The ALP under Bill Shorten appears terrified by the possibility that any independent stance could be portrayed as weakening our defences, so it meekly accepts almost any policy the Coalition advances.

INDIGENOUS AUSTRALIANS

The references in Donald Horne's book to the original Australians reflect general attitudes in the 1960s. The British legal fiction of *terra nullius*, the blatantly absurd claim that the land was unoccupied before the Europeans arrived to take possession of it, was used to justify the alienation of the first Australians from their country. At the time Horne was writing, that legal fiction was backed by what we now see as historical fiction, a narrative implying the Indigenous people had quietly accepted being forcibly integrated into the British Empire. Since then, historians like Henry Reynolds and Lyndall Ryan have corrected the record: violent struggles took place when the original Australians realised that the new arrivals were not prepared to share the land, but were embarking on a course of action that can be described as robbery with violence. Later editions of *The Lucky Country* dealt more fully with the relations between Indigenous Australians and more recent arrivals, recognising the need for the sort of accommodation and proper recognition that New Zealand has with the Māori people through the Treaty of Waitangi, which recognises the prior ownership of the land by Māori people and gives them important legal rights to hunt and fish.

Only a few years after Horne's book was published, the 1967 referendum was overwhelmingly passed, giving Indigenous people full rights of citizenship for the first time since federation. It is often forgotten that South Australia's Indigenous people had full voting rights before 1901, but they lost those rights as one of the conditions imposed on South Australia when they joined the new Commonwealth. Since 1967 there have been several significant steps toward reconciliation with the original Australians. The *Mabo* decision of the High Court established legally the ownership of the land by Indigenous people so long as they had maintained a connection with the land, while the subsequent passing of the *Native Title Act* gave those who still occupy their traditional lands some rights to determine what development is acceptable. When Bob Hawke was prime minister, he canvassed the possibility of negotiating a formal treaty with Indigenous people, broadly along the lines of the Treaty of Waitangi, but this proposal was not supported by his government colleagues.

In 2015, the prime minister Abbott and opposition leader Shorten formally met with a representative group of Indigenous leaders to discuss some form of amendment to the Australian Constitution to recognise the rights of Indigenous people. This was a promising move, as the history of attempts to change the Australian Constitution is sobering; essentially, amendments have been carried only when they have been supported by all the major political parties. It is clear that the Aboriginal and Torres Strait Islander people have diverse views about what might be appropriate. At one end of the spectrum, some want explicit recognition in the Constitution of their prior ownership and a formal treaty with the government acknowledging the injustice of their treatment. At the other end, some felt that they could only hope for some form of advisory body to comment on legislative proposals. This sounded much like the former Aboriginal and Torres Strait Islander Commission, which was abolished by the Howard government. I believe a more reasonable approach is that recommended by an expert panel in 2012, to add a paragraph to the opening section of the Constitution, which now refers just to the establishment of Australia as a federation of the previously existing British colonies. The words they proposed were:

- Recognising that the continent and its islands now known as Australia were first occupied by Aboriginal and Torres Strait Islander peoples;
- Acknowledging the continuing relationship of Aboriginal and Torres Strait Islander peoples with their traditional lands and waters;
- Respecting the continuing cultures, languages and heritage of Aboriginal and Torres Strait Islander peoples;
- Acknowledging the need to secure the advancement of Aboriginal and Torres Strait Islander Peoples;
- The Parliament shall, subject to this Constitution, have power to make laws for the peace, order and good government of the Commonwealth with respect to Aboriginal and Torres Strait Islander peoples.

A significant fraction of those descended from more recent migrants are still in denial about the debt we owe to those who were dispossessed and forcibly alienated from their cultural traditions. On the other hand, many believe we will never be a people at peace with ourselves until we have achieved proper reconciliation with the original Australians.

Kevin Rudd as prime minister in 2008 formally apologised to the 'Stolen Generations' for a practice that had persisted for decades. Successive governments had forcibly removed the children of non-Indigenous fathers from their Indigenous mothers, with the stated aim of assimilating the children into white society. The apology was a significant step toward reconciliation, as is the now common practice of acknowledging the traditional owners of the land at public functions. That being said, rates of incarceration of Indigenous people are about ten times those of their fellow Australians and their average life span is a decade shorter. These are obvious consequences of the alienation of the

Indigenous people from their land. The need remains for the settler society to recognise that we have established our living arrangements at the expense of the Indigenous people, whose culture and identification with country has been violently overthrown. We should also understand that there is much we could learn about the land from its traditional custodians, for whom knowing the country was literally a matter of life and death.

FOOD

Looming shortages

An issue tied closely to our geography that affects everyone is the capacity to produce our food. From the French Revolution to the Arab Spring, lack of food or the inability of large numbers of people to afford food has always been a source of unrest. In 2010, Australian science journalist Julian Cribb wrote *The Coming Famine*. He reviewed studies by international bodies such as the UN's Food and Agriculture Organization as well as scientific groups. The grim reality is that the important indicators of food per person – meat per person, fish per person and grain per person – have all peaked and are all declining. It has been quite a remarkable technical achievement to expand food production since 1900 almost as fast as the human population has grown. In 1900, there were about 2 billion people in the world. Today, there are more than 7 billion, more than double the number when Horne wrote his book. The three-fold expansion of food production in the last hundred years has come partly from technical innovation, but largely from pouring much more energy and other resources into the task. Nearly 40 years ago, one analyst went as far as to describe the modern diet as 'eating oil', an evaluation repeated more recently by author Norman Church.

Only in the last couple of decades have we started losing the battle to produce more food. Cribb warns that we are now losing productive land, partly as a result of past unsustainable use and partly as we take over formerly productive land for human settlements or mineral production. I have watched this process myself in the peri-urban areas around Brisbane. The produce being sold at Brisbane Markets and then bought by consumers at shops or supermarkets now comes from further away than it did 30 years ago. There is no real possibility of producing food from the land that has been concreted over, at least in the short to medium term.

Some changes in our lifestyle and diet have made producing food easier. For example, Australians eat as much beef in total as we did 50 years ago, when the population was about half what it is today. Other changes have made the task more difficult. Between 1970 and 1990, food supplied per person in Sydney doubled! This was not a crash obesity program, although increasing numbers of Australians have become clinically overweight, a consequence of two factors: reduced physical activity and increasing calorie intakes. The main factor driving the increase in how much we eat has been a change in our eating habits. Where most Australians in 1964 bought raw food like meat, fish and vegetables to cook meals, many now buy processed takeaway or microwave meals. When my partner and I moved into a ten-year-old unit on the Sunshine Coast, we noticed that the oven had never been used by any of the previous owners. When you cook your own food, you can choose how much to prepare. If you buy a packaged meal, the quantities are determined for you by the food industry. The hard statistical evidence is that we are eating more food per person. It is also likely that processed food is less nutritious, so we consume larger portions to meet our needs.

GEOGRAPHY

We now face a crisis with several dimensions. Some types of food like fish cannot be produced at will; we farm the seas for our seafood. All of the world's major fisheries are now either at peak production or in decline. The global fish catch has been about 90 million tonnes a year for 30 years, with no real prospect of expansion. Coastal intensive production, known as aquaculture or 'fish farming', is now a significant supplement to the catch; in the last year for which I could find Australian data, the wild catch was about 160,000 tonnes and the farmed fish production about 80,000. Globally, aquaculture has increased from a very low base 30 years ago to about 60 million tonnes. So both locally and globally, it is now a significant fraction of the harvest from the seas.

Back on dry land, climate change is affecting both growing conditions and rainfall, which in turn affects water availability. In many areas of Australia, food production was increased dramatically by irrigation, but that process is now being limited by either water shortages or the salinity caused by that water use. Another critical factor is that cheap fuel is key to agriculture. Farmers now drive tractors and muster livestock on a quad bike, rather than using horses. Importantly, much of the food we eat is no longer sourced from the regions in which we live. A quick trawl around my local supermarket shelves shows that about half the produce there has come from interstate or even overseas. That is only possible as long as we have cheap transport fuels. The decline in availability of oil and its increasing price threatens our ability to both produce and distribute food.

A 2015 report by the insurance organisation Lloyd's, *Food System Shock*, was developed by Anglia Ruskin University's Global Sustainability Institute in the UK, with support from the British and US governments. It predicted that we will face a crisis before 2050. With the world's population projected to keep growing to perhaps reach 9 billion by that date, the increasing demands for food and water supplies appear unmanageable. The report predicts more terrorism and civil wars triggered by a combination of climate change, shortages of food, water and energy, as well as political instability. Australia would not be able to insulate ourselves completely from such upheaval, given how tightly we have knitted ourselves into global systems of production and use.

This raises the broader issue of human health and well-being. A joint study by a commission established by the Rockefeller Foundation and *The Lancet* was also published in 2015. It noted that 'human health is better now than at any time in history' but 'these gains in human health have come at a high price: the degradation of nature's ecological systems on a scale never seen in human history'. Since a 'growing body of evidence shows that the health of humanity is intrinsically linked to the health of the environment', our neglect of the natural environment is putting at risk the health gains made in the last century and even threatening to reverse those gains. This is a warning that we cannot ignore. We urgently need to slow down the impact of human consumption on the natural systems that support life.

Self-sufficiency

One advantage of our geography is that Australia could easily be self-sufficient in food. Even though the shelves of supermarkets groan with imported food, in 2015 we were still exporting more food than we imported. However, to maintain this wealth of food, we must stop degrading productive land. The 1996 *State of the Environment* report estimated that 5 per cent of our grazing land had effectively been sterilised by overuse, while a further 10 per cent needed to be rested by reducing stocking rates for its productivity to be restored.

Successive governments have also been prepared to allow minerals extraction interests to take over productive land. In 2015, the Commonwealth government made the remarkable decision to approve a proposed open-cut coal mine on the Liverpool Plains, which has the extremely productive black soil plains. All around southern Queensland, there are disputes between farmers and the companies wanting to extract coal seam gas. Successive state governments have been so eager to promote the industry that they have given gas companies the right to extract the product regardless of the wishes of the landowner. Farmers worried about the impacts of gas extraction on their land or their groundwater have been told they have no right to object. This in turn has catalysed the amazing development of the Lock the Gate movement, with conservative farmers now actively engaging in acts of civil disobedience to protect their land. The strength of the movement and its level of support in rural areas has led the NSW government to curb the expansion of coal seam gas production in the north of that state, but there has been no such restriction in Queensland.

An additional issue for Queensland comes from UNESCO's warning about the state of the Great Barrier Reef, which requires steps to be taken by the end of 2016 to reduce the run-off of sediment and nutrients from the mainland, a direct consequence of the pattern of land use for agriculture and grazing in the catchments of the coastal rivers. This will probably require both land works to retain sediment and also reduced use of fertilisers and other chemicals that are adding nutrients to the water leaving farms. While it may be possible to achieve those gains without losing production, that seems unlikely; after all, the main reason for using fertiliser and other chemicals is to increase production, so reducing their use is almost certain to cut the output from the land.

There has been some simplistic comment from government sources about the prospect of northern Australia becoming 'the food bowl of Asia'. The 2015–16 budget, despite imposing a wide range of austerity measures on the public sector and its ability to provide services to the community, set aside $2 billion for 'northern development'. This looked likely to repeat previous failed attempts to kick-start agricultural development in northern regions by massive investment of public funds. The Ord River Scheme in Western Australia was promoted as the first big project of this kind several decades ago, providing irrigation water and allowing the production of a wide range of exotic crops for Asian markets. Despite huge public subsidies, the Ord dream has never materialised, so there is no reason to believe that similar projects would be any more successful. As discussed earlier, there are good reasons why the north of Australia is relatively unproductive: its old and nutrient-poor soils, drenching summer rains followed by long dry periods, the pests and diseases that result from a tropical climate, the costs of supplies like fertiliser and pesticides, the local pool of skilled labour and the distance from possible markets for produce. Tipping huge amounts of public money into a few roads and reservoirs is not going to solve those problems. A CSIRO report found that it would be possible to significantly improve agriculture in the north and expand production by modest amounts, but the idea of enlarging it dramatically to become 'the food bowl of Asia' will remain a pipedream.

Evaluating the scale of possible food production from our land raises inevitably the question of population. Australia currently produces about enough food for 50 million people, exporting more than half of that production. Since projections by the Australian Bureau of Statistics show us on a path to a 2100 population of over 60 million, one conclusion is clear.

If we wish to ensure we are able to provide the future food needs of our people, we cannot allow the sort of population growth that results from the present policy settings. So if we are serious about a sustainable future, it is essential that we discuss the question of our future population.

AUSTRALIA AS AN ISLAND NATION

All of human history shows that islands are less likely to be invaded than countries with a land border. One of the few European nations that has not been invaded in recent centuries is the UK, whose most recent security problems were a direct result of the fact that part of that country – Northern Ireland – does share a land border with another country. As in that case, wherever there is a land border there is usually some dispute about where the line sits and the respective rights of people living on either side. The affiliations that are ostensibly religious but actually tribal in Northern Ireland are similar to those in the former Yugoslavia, making it difficult to see any resolution that will be durably peaceful. As in the Middle East, wherever there are two groups of people who both feel they have a legitimate claim to an area of land, there will be an intractable dispute.

Australia was seriously threatened in the 1940s, when Japanese armed forces did plan an invasion with the goal of accessing the resources of this land. Since 1945, our governments have been very enthusiastic to allow those resources to be supplied to other countries in the region, making it relatively unlikely that any of our neighbours would be motivated to launch military action for that reason. It would certainly cause tension if we decided to stop selling our resources, as shown by the reaction when the Gillard government halted live cattle sales to Indonesia in

2011. I can remember when the head of the Australian Atomic Energy Commission, the late Sir Philip Baxter, argued in the early 1970s that Australia should develop nuclear weapons to enable us to defend this country against what he saw as inevitable threats of invasion. As Hugh White has argued, the biggest security threat to Australia probably arises from the possibility that our alignment with the USA will bring us into conflict with our Asian neighbours.

While we have relatively little fear of border disputes, there are obvious tensions that will continue as long as Australia is an island of relative affluence in a region with millions of desperately poor people. The willingness of people to pay thousands of dollars to risk their lives in leaky boats, trying to cross dangerous seas to get here, is a measure of the scale of the problem. The best investment in a secure future would be real and useful aid to the poorest countries, especially those in our region, aimed at ensuring that people feel comfortable where they are. The reduction of our already miserly aid allocation to only about 0.2 per cent of our Gross Domestic Product (GDP), compared with the UN target of 0.7 per cent, is not just shamefully selfish, but also a collective failure to work toward our own future security. A goal of making Australia a truly lucky country would require us to be prepared to share our luck with the poorest people in the world. Floods of refugees from Afghanistan and Iraq are arguably direct consequences of our involvement in ill-judged military operations in those countries. Instability and poverty will continue to motivate people to try to get away from where they are, in search of better lives for them and their children. The problem will certainly be compounded in coming decades by 'climate change refugees', forced to leave Pacific islands or low-lying areas on the Asian mainland and the Indian sub-continent as rising sea levels make their living conditions impossible.

GEOGRAPHY

These looming problems only reinforce Horne's warning that we urgently need a wide-ranging public discussion on what kind of Australia we want to be. The Australia of 2016 is radically different from the country that he described. As he said, rather than being the country that results from random events, we should be trying to create the future we would like to have.

SOCIETY

The republican idea was just one go at what was essential to develop some new sense of identity, some public feeling of being a people who can be described – even if incorrectly – as such-and-such a kind of nation, and act at times as if this were so. This has already happened in creative life ... contemplate where we have come since the 1950s when there was no Australian film industry, little Australian drama, only a few writers, not many historians and scarcely any quality media.

Yet this has not been matched by equal creative activity in economic life or political life. In contemplating our present leaders we come face to face with a paradox ... there are times when the only pragmatic course is to be visionary. But combining a pragmatic style with a workable vision of the future now escapes our political leaders ...
—The Lucky Country, fifth edition, pp. xx–xxi

As Donald Horne lamented 50 years ago and reiterated toward the end of his long and productive life, there is little serious discussion of Australia's future. Barry Jones established the Commission for the Future (CFF) when he was Minister for Science in the Hawke government, but it was never funded or supported at a scale that would have significantly influenced decision-making. When I took a year off from my academic post to direct the CFF in 1988, it had an annual budget of about $1 million and a staff of ten people. It was not supported by Jones's government colleagues or Coalition politicians. I still remember the hostility and ignorance of some elected members when I appeared before the Senate Estimates Committee to defend the CFF's meagre budgetary allocation. A Coalition senator was so opposed ideologically to the idea of thinking about the future that he had clearly not even read the report we were discussing. It was hardly surprising that the CFF's public funding was discontinued when Jones was no longer the responsible minister. It limped along for a few years with limited resources from the private sector, before finally being wound up.

While many Australians have a clear sense of what makes us uniquely Australian, whether it be a sense of fair play or a healthy scepticism, we don't often connect these values to how our institutions and policies should reflect them. Donald Horne blamed our second-rate leaders for not leading these discussions. We should be testing and redeveloping our social institutions, our position on population growth and migration, how our changing social values affect family life, and what changes in the workforce mean for society as a whole. To have these discussions, we must be telling stories in our own voices, and brainstorming alternative futures that we can assess. If you don't know where you want to go, any road will do; if you do know where you would like to be, it is possible to steer in the appropriate direction. That was the aim of the CFF; to remind Australians that there is a wide range of possible futures and stimulate discussion of what sort of country we would like to be in the twenty-first century. That conversation is long overdue.

THE GENERAL QUALITIES OF AUSTRALIANS

It is overly simplistic to ascribe general characteristics to any nation, but we are all shaped to some extent by the social environment in which we grew up. We inevitably internalise what is regarded by those around us as appropriate behaviour. When we travel overseas, we can't help noticing that the behavioural norms in other countries are different. In the introduction to the 1998 fifth edition of his book, Horne wrote that Australia 'should be impelled to display its talents in a sense of reality', observing that we have 'great qualities that could constitute the beginnings of a great nation'. He listed what he regarded as these qualities:

- anti-doctrinaire tolerance
- a sense of fair play
- a sense of family
- an interest in nature
- adaptability

- fraternalism
- scepticism
- a talent for improvisation
- courage and stoicism.

It would still be possible to mount an argument that these qualities are likely to be found in that hypothetical character 'the average Australian'.

I feel more comfortable in my native country of Australia than I do in other countries because of the scepticism, tolerance and sense of fair play which are still obvious here. When Tony Abbott and Joe Hockey launched what amounted to class warfare with their government's first budget in 2014, the response from the community was overwhelming. Even those who would have benefited from the largesse to high earners mostly saw the budget as unfair and the government's level of support in opinion polls sank like a lead bag. Australians tend to be stoic and put up with conditions that cause visitors to complain bitterly, whether the conditions are under human control like the state of the public transport system, or totally beyond our control like the weather. We also tend to be sceptical of dogmatic politicians. Voters in 1993 saw John Hewson as driven by ideology and rejected his bid for the prime ministership. John Howard was arguably more ideological, but he was more careful about hiding it until he got control of the Senate; that emboldened him to launch into the WorkChoices policy, which was widely seen as an attack on working people. It was the beginning of the end for his parliamentary career.

Some of these characteristics have been deliberately eroded in recent decades. The Hawke, Keating and Howard governments all adopted a policy of selling public enterprises to the private sector and encouraging citizens to become shareholders.

So institutions like the postal service, airports and the utilities providing electricity and water are now seen as commercial operations expected to meet profit targets rather than provide basic services equitably. The sense of fair play has also been eroded by systematically diverting resources from public schools to elite private schools, reducing the chance that the talented child of poor parents will be able to develop their potential.

Comparisons with countries that have not adopted the extreme economic approach of Australia, the UK and the USA are revealing. Denmark, as one example of a small country with relatively few natural resources but an egalitarian approach, had in 2015 a minimum wage of $20 an hour, a 33-hour working week, free health care, free child care and free university education. To fund those services, the taxation levels are higher and most pay their taxes. By comparison, Australia had at that time a minimum wage of $17.29 an hour, a 38-hour working week and a system in which we pay for health care, child care and education. Australia does not just have lower taxes but also has much more generous treatment of large corporations and wealthy individuals; the extreme example is that there are people on the *Business Review Weekly* Rich 200 List with declared incomes so low they pay no tax, and in some cases are even exempt from the Medicare levy! Living on my university pension and earnings from my writing, I pay the Medicare levy, so I am almost incandescent with rage at the thought that millionaires are paying nothing.

A recent book, *Northern Lights: The Positive Policy Example of Sweden, Finland, Denmark and Norway* by Andrew Scott, argued that we should be improving our social institutions by following the Scandinavian examples, rather than systematically eroding them toward US standards. I have great sympathy for that argument, having seen the alarming increase in homeless people sleeping rough in recent years and having experienced the insecurity that results in other countries from having large numbers of desperate people on the streets. It was noteworthy that the 2015 UN report on progress toward sustainability put the four leading nations as Norway, Sweden, Denmark and Finland, while the USA ranked 29th of the 34 OECD nations. So why do so many of our politicians see the USA as an exemplar to which we should aim, rather than the much more successful Scandinavian nations?

As well as significant changes to the fairness of Australian society, there have been changes to our tolerance of difference. Some of these changes are positive, like the dramatic shift in attitudes toward same-sex relationships, which were illegal in 1964, became seen as acceptable in the 1990s and are now broadly accepted, with polls showing a clear majority in favour of allowing same-sex couples to marry. If I had been writing this book ten years ago I would have noted the shift of Australia from being a country in which the Christian churches dominated social and ethical thinking to one which was much more diverse and not just accepting of a wide range of other religions, but also more positive about people having no religious beliefs. A visit to the USA is in that sense like going through a time-warp back to the Australia of the 1960s; it is almost impossible to be elected to any public office without expressing strong religious beliefs. The fanning by some Australian politicians of concern about Muslims has led to some very unpleasant public expressions of intolerance toward Islam in particular, leading in turn to increasing social tension.

SECOND-RATE LEADERS?

Donald Horne wrote about 'second-rate' leaders oblivious to the changes around them. I heard a colleague say recently that it would take a very generous assessor to give some of the present crop of elected politicians that *high* a rating. A US comedy show even put together a collection of clips of the former Australian prime minister Tony Abbott, extending from his startling admission that he was not 'the suppository of all wisdom' to his stony-faced silence when asked a question he had difficulty answering in a glib three-word slogan. The palpable sense of relief around the nation when he was displaced by Malcolm Turnbull was an indication of the unease felt even by some of those who had voted for Abbott; one commentator quipped that the whole nation had a case of buyer's remorse when we realised who we had elected in 2013.

The 2015 ABC documentary *The Killing Season* reminded voters of the dysfunctional aspects of the ALP governments between 2007 and 2013. Kevin Rudd was elected with high hopes and raised community expectations with his wonderful apology to the Stolen Generations and his engagement of forward thinkers in his 2020 Summit. But he became a victim of his failure to delegate responsibility to his ministers and to involve his colleagues in critical strategic decisions, leading to a loss of confidence in his leadership and his removal from office by his party. While Julia Gillard was in many ways a remarkably effective prime minister who achieved significant advances despite her tenuous grip on office, she was always struggling against the negative perceptions of the way she came to the leadership, sexist attacks by shock-jocks and the relentless campaign by Kevin Rudd to regain the leadership.

The way the parliamentary ALP was shown to operate by that documentary illustrates a general problem which afflicts contemporary politics. It was equally visible in the campaign run by Tony Abbott and his supporters to undermine Malcolm Turnbull's first leadership stint and install Abbott as opposition leader, as well as the mirror-image campaign run by Turnbull's supporters to return the favour by removing Abbott from the prime ministership. With the conspicuous exception of Turnbull, very few of our current political leaders had any significant record of achievement before they entered politics. It was once expected that people would go into politics after a successful career of some sort that gave them real-world experience. Most contemporary politicians have moved from full-time education into a union office or a party job or a role on a politician's staff, so their only real skill is playing the political game. As the adage goes, if you only have a hammer, every problem looks like a nail.

This political generation sees even a problem like climate change as a political issue, one of weighing up the costs and benefits of different actions against the way it will influence voters in the marginal electorates. So focus groups and frequent polling shape their responses. Having swept to office after a campaign in which he described climate change as the greatest moral challenge of our time, Rudd was persuaded to drop his proposed package of actions when the backroom boys of the NSW ALP told him that it was being badly received in the western suburbs of Sydney. This understandably caused the electorate to wonder what Rudd stood for, if he was prepared to abandon the greatest moral challenge of our time when spooked by the latest polling. The collapse in Rudd's apparent support caused the party room to panic and overthrow him in what was effectively a dramatic late-night coup d'état.

A party room that understood that you can't negotiate with natural systems and that you need a concerted policy response to a problem like climate change might have behaved differently. This is a completely bipartisan comment. Tony Abbott and his supporters, most prominently the now-retired senator

Nick Minchin, undermined the leadership of Malcolm Turnbull precisely because he had recognised that the Liberal Party needed a coherent response to climate change. Turnbull had negotiated with Kevin Rudd to water down his package of measures to a point where the Coalition promised bipartisan support. Minchin was actively in denial about the science of climate change. The ABC documentary *Madlands* showed him travelling the world with activist Anna Rose, desperately trying to find credible support for his prejudices. He went beyond the normal political role in trying to undermine public confidence in the science. He and Abbott harnessed the lunar right of the Liberal Party, many of whom are still in denial about climate change decades after the science was established to the satisfaction of those who understand it, to precipitate a leadership spill. In a three-way contest between Turnbull, Abbott and Joe Hockey, Abbott defeated Turnbull by one vote in a run-off after Hockey was eliminated – with one of Turnbull's known supporters ill and unable to vote. The whole exercise, like the late-night removal of Rudd, looked more like the sort of squabble that infected student politics than the behaviour of a serious political party.

In early 2015, the public standing of politicians had sunk to an all-time low. The prime minister and the leader of the opposition were competing for the dubious honour of being the more unpopular of the two, with both having more voters disapproving of their performance than approving. Tony Abbott's simplistic three-word slogans and constant negativity were very effective as a leader of the opposition, but he was totally incapable of being an effective prime minister. This was underlined early in 2015 when two backbenchers moved a 'spill motion', effectively to declare the leadership vacant even though there was no rival candidate, and attracted 39 votes in the party room for their vote of no confidence in the prime minister. He was effectively given six months to lift his game. When his party concluded that he was unable to change, they voted for his removal. This was an extraordinary step, as the Coalition had been so virulent in their criticism of the ALP when they removed Kevin Rudd from the post of prime minister. In Shorten's case, his tangled syntax and laboured style led one comedian to lampoon each week his latest 'zinger', suggesting that he lacks the gravitas expected of a national leader. Both Abbott and Shorten seemed more interested in making cheap political points than setting out a vision of the future Australia they wanted to work toward, reinforcing Donald Horne's despairing comment about our leaders. As discussed earlier, the replacement of Abbott by Turnbull and his assurance that he would not be continuing his predecessor's simplistic slogans was greeted with widespread relief by supporters of all the major political parties, reflecting a hope that we might see a more intelligent approach to political issues.

STRONG SOCIAL INSTITUTIONS

We still have strong social institutions, although these have been significantly eroded since 1964. As one concrete example, at that time it was still regarded as an unforgivable offence for ministers to mislead parliament. As prime minister, Gough Whitlam sacked ministers for this fault, even when they had inadvertently misled the House by simply repeating advice from the relevant department. There were at least two instances of federal ministers misleading parliament in the short period while I was writing this book, but no sanctions resulted. The instance that caused most comment was foreign minister Julie Bishop telling the parliament in May 2015 that a letter written by Lindt Café siege gunman

Man Haron Monis had been provided to the inquiry into that incident. A week later she admitted that it had not.

A second example is the traditional separation of powers between the different arms of government: the legislature which passes laws, the executive which implements them and the judiciary which adjudicates disputes. This was always a difficult concept for some state governments. The then premier of Queensland, Joh Bjelke-Petersen, was famously unable to explain it at the Fitzgerald Inquiry. The more recent Newman government aroused the hostility of most of the legal profession when they elevated a magistrate to the post of chief justice, in a move widely seen as trying to make the judiciary more compliant. In mid-2015, the Abbott government canvassed a proposal that a minister would be able to cancel an individual's citizenship without any right of judicial review of the decision. *Crikey* pointed out that if the prime minister believed that approach to be appropriate, he would give the wrong answer to one of the questions on the government's own citizenship test! The proposed changes were referred to a parliamentary committee, then extensively amended and eventually passed with bi-partisan support.

Our social institutions have been further weakened by politicising the public service. The Westminster tradition was that the public service was apolitical and gave fearless advice to ministers, who then made decisions taking into account the political implications. The staff in each department were expected to have expertise in that area: transport, health, education etc. As a result, when the government changed there was relatively little impact on the public service. Departments usually scanned the policy pronouncements of the contending parties at an election and prepared two sets of briefing notes, one for an incoming Coalition government and the other to be used after an ALP win.

Up until the 1990s, this process was honoured most of the time. The Howard government elected in 1996 changed the public service fundamentally. First, they removed most of the department heads who had advised the previous Keating and Hawke governments, replacing them with people who were seen as ideologically aligned with the Coalition. Second, they imported the notion of generic management, believing that running a department did not require any specific expertise. So a Health bureaucrat could be put in charge of Education or Transport, as long as they were ideologically sympathetic to the government. These two changes have systematically weakened the quality of advice given to ministers, which is a quite fundamental problem. The system of parliamentary democracy works on the basis that ministers have the political sensitivity to weigh up the implications of a decision on the electorate, but they are not expected to have tecÿical expertise in the area of their portfolio. We don't expect the Minister for Education to be an experienced educator or the Minister for the Arts to have a performing background, so they need to be advised by departmental officials who *do* have the appropriate expertise. That is less likely now than it was in 1964.

There was also in 2015 widespread discussion of the electoral system. The Senate, with equal numbers of senators from each state, was established at the time of federation to ensure that the national parliament would not be dominated totally by the more populous states. The system of proportional representation was adopted for the Senate elections to ensure that significant minorities would be represented. When most people voted either for the ALP or its conservative opponents, the system led inevitably to almost all the senators coming from those parties. Senate elections became more complicated when significant minority parties came onto the scene. By the 2013 election, the vote was being split about 40 per cent each to the ALP and the Coalition parties, about 10 per cent to the Greens and about 10 per cent to other candidates. This resulted in a group of senators being elected from so-called micro-parties, benefiting from the steady accumulation of preferences as other candidates were eliminated. While most voters in South Australia had heard of Nick Xenophon, who had been an independent member of the state parliament elected on an anti–poker machine platform before entering national politics, most electors in Victoria had never heard of the Motoring Enthusiast Party, while there was speculation in New South Wales that some voters had confused the Liberal Democratic Party with the Liberal Party. For whatever reason, the government elected in 2013 found itself having to negotiate with ten Green senators and eight other cross-benchers to pass its legislation. While many observers thought the Abbott government had been saved from significant electoral trouble by the reluctance of the Senate to pass its more extreme proposals, there was growing concern that the electoral system could be making the task of governing much more difficult by almost ensuring that the elected government will have a complex and hostile Senate to deal with. This problem provoked calls to reform the electoral system to set a minimum primary vote for a candidate to be elected, but such a change would require the unlikely support of the existing Senate.

MIGRATION AND POPULATION

At the time Horne wrote his book, Australia was still a predominantly Anglo-Celtic nation. I grew up thinking Australia was a transplanted form of England, but later reflection showed me that there are many obvious elements of that Australia which were derived from Scotland, Ireland and Wales. The education system was much more like the Scottish model than the English, as were such features as pipe bands and the existence of a public golf course in most small towns; my local golf course was actually called a links, the original Scottish term for the sandy wasteland between the sea and pastures, even though we were a very long way from the sea. The strong union tradition and the level of support for republicanism were more like Ireland and Wales than England. The nearest large town had the Welsh tradition of an annual eisteddfod, at which I had my first experience of public speaking and choral singing.

The years since the end of World War II had seen significant migration from western Europe, predominantly from the UK but with large groups from Italy and Greece and smaller numbers from northern and eastern parts of Europe. These were people who had endured catastrophic wartime conditions in Europe and were seeking at least a more peaceful life, if not necessarily a more prosperous one. Large numbers of British migrants were attracted by a scheme which offered them transport to Australia for the extraordinarily small amount of ten pounds, probably equivalent to about $100 in today's purchasing power; two of our recent prime ministers, Abbott and Gillard, are the descendants of these 'ten-pound Poms' as they were universally known.

There were also significant groups of migrants from other countries. I remember that there was a large Estonian community in a small country town near where I was growing up in the 1950s. As in other countries, migrants tended to go to the area where they knew somebody, leading to concentrations like the Italians in the Melbourne suburb of Carlton. Many of these people retain a very strong connection to and identification with the country their parents or grandparents left to come here. There were wild celebrations in the streets of Carlton when Italy won the soccer World Cup in 1982 and again in 2006.

Rapid population growth

The high level of migration has given Australia a rate of population growth that is unusually rapid for an affluent nation. In 1945, Australia and Sweden both had populations of about 7 million. Today, Sweden has about 9 million people and Australia about 23 million. Economists and politicians generally favour population growth because they think it is good for the economy. There is no doubt that a larger population benefits some sectors, most obviously housing, retail and land development, but there is a vigorous debate about whether the overall benefits outweigh the costs.

The discussion is confused by superficial comments about the birthrate. When *The Lucky Country* was written, the average Australian woman had four children, so the birthrate was contributing to rapid population increase. Since women gained control over their fertility, the birthrate has dropped spectacularly and is now on average about 1.9 children per adult woman. This is less than the replacement rate, leading to some uninformed comments that the population would be declining if it were not for immigration. In fact, the natural increase – births minus deaths – has consistently been above 120,000 a year and at the time of writing was about 150,000 a year. The reason is that the past birthrate and net inward migration together mean that the number of adult women of reproductive age is still increasing.

Demographic studies show that if we have zero net migration from today, the natural increase will slow as the population ages, with the population stabilising sometime in the 2030s at about 28 million. If we have relatively low levels of net migration, the population would stabilise later at a higher level. Any level of net migrant intake up to about 70,000 a year allows the future population to stabilise eventually. This is because approximately

70,000 people leave Australia in an average year, so zero net migration would allow about 70,000 people to come in. To put that in perspective, our recent refugee quota has been less than 20,000, so an overall figure of 70,000 would still allow choices about a more generous refugee policy, provision for family reunion and possibly even small numbers of skilled migrants if there were to be critical job shortages. The recent migration level, about 250,000 a year, has Australia on target for a 2100 population of more than 60 million. Just as today's Australia of 23 million people is radically different from the 1964 country of about 10 million, so a future country with 60 million people would be radically different socially, economically and environmentally from the country we live in today.

Given the significance of today's population policy for the long-term future of Australia, it is surprising and alarming that it gets such perfunctory and superficial attention from politicians and the mass media. I wrote a book, *Bigger or Better?*, about the population debate in 2012. The book gained me many invitations to discuss the population question on ABC radio. The issues also got a lot of attention at writers' festivals and ideas festivals, but the discussion has done little to change national policy, which is still effectively 'the more the better', in Bob Hawke's words. The rapid population increase has directly caused an infrastructure crisis in our cities, which in turn is causing resentment and blaming of identifiable migrants, producing social tensions which some politicians have deliberately inflamed for cynical political gain.

We could easily stabilise our future population if we chose to do so. Yet the recent approach of allowing approximately 250,000 migrants a year assumes we are happy to have the population expand until it causes critical shortages or social unrest. That is not a clever approach.

Complex migration considerations

Today, nearly half of the entire Australian population was either born overseas or has at least one parent born overseas. No other country has recent migrants being such a huge fraction of its population; the only one that comes close is Israel. There is no doubt that Australia is much more diverse and consequently a much more interesting country now than it was when Donald Horne wrote his book. It is also true that the rate of growth in recent years has caused a range of problems. Recent migrants are much more likely to have come from Asia or the Middle East. While some of the change has been accommodated in a remarkably peaceful way, with obvious benefits in terms of the diversity of urban areas in particular, the fact that many of the recent arrivals come with significantly different values has inevitably been a source of tension. Radio shock-jocks and some politicians have used inflammatory language to stir up hostility toward recent migrants, culminating in the very disturbing so-called Cronulla Riots of 2005.

In the current political climate, it has become almost impossible to have a serious discussion about the scale of migration or its social impacts, because it is a complex question. Criticism of the growth rate can be coded racism, or can be misinterpreted as concealing a racist agenda. Some of the problems are simply a function of the strain on urban development by increased numbers. But some of the tension is caused by differences in values: different religions, different views about the role of women, different expectations about family size and so on. Most politicians favour rapid population growth because of the widespread delusion that this is good for the economy; when Kevin Rudd was prime minister, he responded to a question about a projection showing the population heading for 36 million by saying he believed in 'a big Australia'. A political insider said, in reference to the angry response, 'the focus groups went ballistic'. For a time after that incident, politicians made more measured comments, implying they shared the community concerns. But it was largely cosmetic rhetoric.

Some politicians have been prepared to walk both sides of the street, supporting large-scale migration in the professed belief that it brings economic benefits while simultaneously inciting hostility toward the individual migrants. One of the most egregious examples is Scott Morrison, who has a determination for self-promotion that is remarkable even by the standards of elected politicians. When he was opposition spokesperson on immigration in 2010, Morrison boasted in a published article that the Howard government had increased net inwards migration to nearly 250,000 people in its last year in office. He said that this policy was designed to achieve positive economic outcomes and so it demonstrated the superior economic management of Coalition governments. In the very same article, he attacked the then ALP government for allowing similar levels of migration, accusing it of being out of touch with community opinion. It takes some flexibility and chutzpah to attack the government for its migration policy while boasting for having taken an identical approach when his party was in power, but that was Morrison's strategy.

When Julia Gillard replaced Kevin Rudd as prime minister in 2010, she was quick to distance herself from what were seen as his less popular policy stances: his support for a tax on the most profitable mining ventures and his championing of rapid population growth. Where Rudd had renamed the traditional portfolio of Immigration by appointing a Minister for Population, Gillard went a step further and re-badged Tony Burke as Minister for Sustainable Population. While this was presumably intended to signal to the electorate a less enthusiastic approach to high levels of net inwards migration, the interpretation within Canberra circles was that the portfolio encompassed the distribution of the migrants as well as their numbers. This could have been a signal that decentralisation, a topic of political discussion several decades ago, was back on the agenda. However, in the three years between the renaming of the office and the loss of power by the ALP, there was no sign of action to influence where migrants go when they arrive in Australia. While the labour needs of the mining industry are often advanced to justify high levels of migration, few migrants move to the regions where mining is conducted. Most new migrants understandably settle in the largest cities where they are most likely to find communities in which they feel comfortable. It is possible in principle to attach conditions to visas for skilled migrants, precluding them from working in the major cities, but this approach has not been taken by recent Australian governments. With the return of Rudd to the prime ministership, Tony Burke's title reverted to Minister for Immigration.

After the election of the Abbott government, Scott Morrison became Minister for Immigration and Border Control. The new title sent a clear message to these voters who were concerned about migration levels that the government was determined to police our borders and keep people out. While the government used the line in public of 'refusing to comment on operational matters', navy personnel were being used to turn back boats carrying refugees. In 2015, evidence emerged that public funds were also being used to bribe people-smugglers to return to Indonesia with their human cargo; this extraordinary action was implicitly justified by the then prime minister when he said that keeping out unwanted migrants was so important that such means were acceptable. Ironically, while these measures were being trumpeted as demonstrating the capacity of the government to control our borders, the level of net inward migration remained above 250,000 a year. The overwhelming majority of those entering Australia were 'skilled migrants' who were claimed to be bringing in abilities not to be found in the local workforce, or 'business migrants' who would establish new enterprises and employ local people. There is very little evidence that is happening, while there is a perception that cashed-up business migrants are driving city house prices out of the reach of many workers. While the law says that foreigners can only buy new properties, a 2015 *Four Corners* documentary showed that there is widespread evasion of this requirement. The perception that migrants and foreign citizens are driving up house prices is generating a new level of hostility toward migrants.

There is no sign of the community discussing 'what the whole place is about', as Horne called for in 1964. Urban Australia has changed dramatically, so that anyone walking the streets of our capital cities or catching public transport can hardly fail to notice that our population has become much more diverse. The Anglo-Celtic nation where young Donald grew up has been transformed into a multicultural Australia in which over 100 languages are spoken, even if most of them are not formally taught or their use encouraged.

What I notice as I move around Australia is that country towns and regional areas are not as diverse as the large cities. I swim as well as play cricket and golf on the Sunshine Coast and the Fleurieu Peninsula in South Australia; in those activities, you would notice little change from 1964 except that there are now more people around. The diversity you can't help noticing in Brisbane has not spread to Buderim or Bundaberg; the diversity you can't help noticing in Adelaide has barely spread to Aldinga. The establishment of SBS meant that news broadcasts became available in a wide range of community languages, but the mainstream has not embraced that diversity. SBS viewer numbers remain small, so the Abbott government felt able to abandon its explicit pre-election promise not to cut the funds allocated to the multicultural service. In 2015, parliament was even urged to change the law to allow SBS to show more advertising, justifying the move by arguing that the government's budget cuts would otherwise lead to reduced services. SBS staff campaigned against the move and the parliament decided to reduce funding of SBS rather than allow them to accept greater amounts of advertising.

URBAN DEVELOPMENT

The Sydney in which Donald Horne lived was a much smaller and more compact city than any of today's urban areas. I lived in the city at that time. Like almost all residents, I lived within comfortable walking distance of public transport: in my case, at different times I lived near railway stations, tram stops and bus stops. The city was essentially organised around its public transport system, since relatively few people had cars and even fewer drove to work. But the era of near-universal car ownership was arriving. This allowed the development of sprawling outer suburbs that did not have any public transport, assuming that the residents would drive. As in north America, the availability of large areas of land has led to large building blocks and large houses; at more than 210 square metres, the average new house in Australia is now the largest in the world.

Short-term economics has driven changes in land use. When I moved to Brisbane in 1980, the area near where I lived in the southern suburbs was surrounded by orchards and market gardens. They have all been replaced by housing. One orchardist explained his decision to me: the value of his land for housing was so high that he was financially better off selling the land, retiring and spending his time fishing and playing golf than he had been working 16 hours a day in his orchard. The long-term problem is that the food-producing land has been concreted over, so the food for our cities now comes from further away, at greater cost and requiring more resources for transport and processing.

Transport

Today, our cities rival the sprawling US settlements like Phoenix, Arizona, as the least densely occupied urban areas on the planet. Greater Brisbane, with its 2 million or so inhabitants, spreads over about the same area as Greater London, with about 8 million, or Tokyo with 12 million. Those cities have good public transport all the way out to the urban fringe, but even with goodwill it would be impossible to provide the same services in the Brisbane area with so many fewer customers. Where good public transport is provided, as with the Sydney or Brisbane ferries, people use it. Brisbane's large investment in busways, to provide buses with a dedicated artery, has dramatically improved the speed and reliability of bus services and attracted many commuters out of their cars. The first busway saw something like a million extra passengers on the bus routes using it in its first year of operation.

The transport problem for our cities is accentuated by the political feedback loop. More commuters use the car than public transport, so most politicians lean toward funding roads rather than trains or buses or trams. When new roads are built, they make car journeys faster and so more people choose to drive. The problem with the road-building approach is that it is inevitably only a short-term solution. Every time a new road is built, it attracts traffic until it becomes inadequate, provoking demands for another new road or a widening of the existing one. Even though no city in the world has ever solved the traffic problem by building more roads, Australian urban authorities seem determined to repeat the mistakes of north America. In the extreme example of Los Angeles, half the central business district is devoted to the car, but there is still gridlock every morning and every afternoon. Many overseas cities now have systems of road charging to discourage driving into the central areas.

Of course, no two cities are the same, and different decisions have led to different outcomes. In the 1960s, there was a trend of thinking that trams were old-fashioned. Sydney and Brisbane got rid of their entire tram systems, while Adelaide kept just one tram line from Glenelg to the western edge of the CBD. Melbourne was at the time more conservative and kept its system of tramways. As a result, it now has a much better public transport system than the other Australian cities. Trams are now making a comeback as 'light rail'. Adelaide has extended the Glenelg line, first to the eastern end of the CBD and then beyond to the Entertainment Centre. Sydney built one line from Central Station to Darling Harbour, then extended that line to the inner western suburbs and is planning for a major route from the city to the eastern suburbs. The Gold Coast has a light rail from the beaches to its hospital, with a 2015 announcement to extend the line to Helensvale train station, allowing Brisbane people to get to the beach by public transport. Canberra is planning a new light rail system. The obvious advantage of trams and trains is that they carry many more people per metre of transport corridor than can be moved by car. Buses are also much more effective at moving people than cars, but in most of our urban areas they are slowed by sharing road space with cars. Sydney and Brisbane now have rail links to their airports, giving both more efficient and more reliable travel.

When Sydney was chosen to host the 2000 Olympic Games, planners realised that rail would be the only way to move the large crowds expected at the Homebush site. A special spur line was constructed and has proved to be extremely effective. Perth has built two new rail lines north and south of the CBD. The clever move of putting the rail lines down the middle of freeways has provided car users with daily demonstrations of the benefits of using the train. I was told by WA transport expert Professor Peter Newman that the development has dramatically changed the housing market, with rational people prepared to pay more to live within walking distance of a station to enable a civilised trip to the city rather than a stressful drive.

The major problem with urban infrastructure in general, and public transport in particular, is the issue of funding. Dr Jane O'Sullivan of the University of Queensland has calculated that the costs to the community of each extra person is about a quarter of a million dollars. State and local governments everywhere in Australia are in desperate trouble meeting the demands of our rapidly growing population. This leads to pressure to sell public assets or put together improbable public–private partnerships to try to meet the needs. Although public transport has improved in recent decades in all our major cities, the improvements have not kept pace with the growing needs of the increasing urban populations. So there is a widespread community perception, in my view an accurate one, that the quality of life in our cities is declining as the provision of critical services fails to keep pace with the growth in the urban population.

A second, and equally serious problem, is the changing nature of employment. The railway systems of our cities, as well as Melbourne's tramways and most bus networks, are radial systems devised to bring workers from the suburbs to the city centre. But the pattern of work has changed very significantly. Office work is no longer confined to the central business district, with many businesses choosing to take advantage of cheaper office space in the suburbs. That relocation forces most of their employees and customers to drive. The same has happened to retail trade. When Donald Horne wrote his book, most of the large stores were concentrated in the central area, so people went into the city to do their shopping. In the last 50 years, with most people having cars, large suburban shopping centres have gradually taken over the retail business. Most are surrounded by huge car parks and so most customers arrive by car. In general, these centres are not well served by public transport, so that change in shopping behaviour has reinforced the move to car-based cities.

As well as improving public transport, the twenty-first century has seen a renewed enthusiasm for inner-city living. A significant fraction of all new urban dwellings are now flats or home units near the city or a major transport node, allowing people to live without a car and either use public transport or walk to work. There has also been a revival of cycling. Where there are quite civilised cities in western Europe in which 30 to 40 per cent of all urban journeys are made by bicycle, in Australia it has been seen as only for children and teenagers until they are old enough to drive or ride a motorbike. Now our cities are building bike paths and marking bike lanes on roads, allowing cyclists to move around in relative safety. A city like Adelaide, with wide streets and comparatively flat land, is ideally suited to cycling, so the resurgence is understandable.

Infrastructure

Most politicians support rapid growth because they believe it is good for the economy. In fact, that belief overlooks one critical factor: the infrastructure demands of a growing population. In my 2012 book *Bigger or Better?* I reviewed the analysis by

Dr Jane O'Sullivan, using simple maths to show that there is a serious problem. The average age of built infrastructure is about 50 years. Some lasts more like a century, but some needs to be replaced after 20 or 30 years, so 50 is a reasonable average. The pipes, roads and bridges need on average to be replaced about every 50 years, so the replacement bill is about one-fiftieth of the capital value of the infrastructure, or 2 per cent. If the population is increasing by 1 per cent a year, we need to add to the standard replacement bill of 2 per cent an additional 1 per cent for the extra people, making the bill 3 per cent of the capital value — one and a half times what it would have been if the population were stable. In other words, a 1 per cent growth rate inflates by 50 per cent the infrastructure bill, but it only increases revenue by 1 per cent.

Australia's population growth rate in recent years has been as high as 1.8 per cent, which is extraordinary for a developed country; it is about three times the average growth rate in the OECD, the club of relatively affluent nations. With the steady drift from regional areas to capital cities, the large urban areas have been growing by about 2 per cent a year. The same maths shows that a 2 per cent growth rate actually doubles the infrastructure bill, but only increases revenue by 2 per cent at best. The situation is made even worse by the fact that much of the internal migration does not cross state borders. When people move from rural Queensland to the south-east corner, they do not add anything to the state's revenue, but they impose an extra cost burden. Predictably in this situation, every state government in Australia, with the possible exception of Tasmania, which is blessed with a lower growth rate, is struggling to balance the budget while meeting the increasing demands of their growing urban populations. This is causing social strains as well as political instability, as disgruntled voters throw out governments failing to meet their needs, only to find the replacement administration equally unable to solve the problem. Brisbane has tried to cope with an orgy of building roads, tunnels and bridges. This has turned large areas of the inner suburbs into oppressive concrete jungles, without really solving the transport problems. It has also created serious public finance issues as the cobbled-together public–private partnerships struggle to keep their revenue heads above the rising waters of costs. Some of these arrangements have predictably failed to meet the over-ambitious revenue forecasts, so the hybrid entities have collapsed. Bailing them out with public money has put further burdens on state government finances.

In 2015, the rate of population growth was measurably slowing. High unemployment had made moving to Australia appear less attractive to potential migrants, so net migration was projected to drop from the recent level of about 250,000 a year to something like 160,000. The unemployment rate in Australia is now higher than in the USA, so one observer said, 'Why would you move to another country when you won't be able to get a job there?' Economists and the governor of the Reserve Bank expressed concern that the growth rate for 2014 had 'only' been 1.4 per cent, which is still double the average for affluent countries. It was described as 'a danger signal for an already faltering economy'. James McIntyre, who is the head of economic research at Macquarie Group and a former Treasury official, said, 'It's another challenge for policy makers already struggling with a difficult situation.' Tim Toohey, chief economist for Goldman Sachs in Australia, was quoted as saying, 'This suggests the Australian economy will likely fall short of the current growth path expected by policy makers in the near term.' These comments are a reminder that the Australian economy depends critically on population growth to increase consumption. They are also a reminder of the continuing obsession economists have with maintaining the rate of economic growth, seeing it as the critical indicator of progress.

As I discussed in *Bigger or Better?* the fundamental political problem is that the Commonwealth government makes the decisions which directly affect the rate of population growth, such as migration quotas and incentives for Australian women to have children. A growing population means that the overall size of the economy will grow, even with inadequate economic management, so the government can portray itself to the electorate in a good light. The task of providing the necessary roads, public transport, schools and health care facilities falls to state and territory governments, whose revenues are not adequate for the task. The so-called fiscal imbalance between the Commonwealth and the states has caused many observers to say that the model of our federal system needs to be revised, perhaps giving the states and territories increased capacity to levy their own taxes and charges. The reality of day-to-day politics, in which elected representatives are eager to take credit for spending and very reluctant to accept responsibility for raising revenue, makes a resolution seem improbable. In the absence of a fundamental change, the cities will continue to respond inadequately to the needs of growing urban populations and the social tensions will accelerate.

CHANGING SOCIAL VALUES

Religion

One of the most striking changes since 1964 has been the decline of the importance of religion and the political influence of churches. The Australia of the 1960s was one in which over

95 per cent of people formally identified with Christianity. My school roll recorded each child as being Church of England, Roman Catholic or one of the smaller Protestant denominations: Methodist, Presbyterian, Church of Christ, Baptist, Congregationalist and so on.

I grew up in a small town of about 1,000 people. It had four different Protestant churches. The only other places where people could meet were the milk bar and the hall owned by the Country Women's Association. Almost everyone who married did so in church, and funerals were invariably church ceremonies. Church leaders were routinely asked for their opinions about ethical and moral issues. On some occasions, the churches weighed in on political debates and explicitly urged their congregations to vote for or against particular parties. On Sundays hardly anybody worked, shops and pubs were closed, there was little organised sport and in some areas even the swings in children's playgrounds were locked up to deter people from 'defiling the Sabbath'.

Anyone who visits the USA, where it would be almost impossible for a person who rejected religion to be elected to any sort of public office, gets a glimpse back into that earlier phase of Australian life. The changes have been gradual over the 50 years, but they represent such a fundamental change that Roy Williams's 2015 book *Post-God Nation* is devoted entirely to how Australia came to forsake religion. The recent revelations about sexual abuse of young people have certainly reinforced the trend, but it was unmistakeable long before those matters came to light. In Donald Horne's time, nobody would have dared to suggest in public that religious people were acting immorally and colluding to protect perpetrators of serial abuse of children, although we now know that was happening.

Families

As discussed earlier, Australian women are now on average having fewer children. Where four or five were quite usual when I was young, many modern families consist of a couple with one or two children. A related issue is that divorce is now much more readily available than it was in 1964. About 40 per cent of marriages now end in divorce. There is no reason to believe that people are more likely to enter into unsuitable marriages now than they were 50 years ago, so it is safe to conclude that there were then many people unhappily trapped in marriages from which there was no easy escape. The establishment in the 1970s by the Whitlam government of the Family Law Court made it easier and less expensive to end unsatisfactory marriages. In a way, the passage of that legislation was an early indication of the declining power of the churches, which broadly campaigned against the changes by appealing to the traditional injunction in the marriage service that those whom 'God had joined together in holy matrimony' could not be 'put asunder'. It would be comforting to think that the easier availability of divorce will have reduced the frequency of women being trapped in violent domestic situations, but Australian women are still being killed or seriously injured by their male domestic partners at an alarming rate of about one a week.

Society is today much more tolerant than it was in 1964 of couples living together without being legally married. Again, that is a reflection of the declining importance of the churches' disapproval of what was known in 1964 as 'living in sin'. We are also much more tolerant of homosexuality, which was still regarded as a criminal offence when Donald Horne wrote his book, whereas there is now majority acceptance of the idea of same-sex marriage. So there is much more diversity in what is regarded as a typical household today. Where a suburban street in 1964 almost always consisted of an unbroken line of houses each containing a married couple with about four children, today it is much more likely to have a diverse mix of married and unmarried, straight and gay, with children and without. As discussed earlier, the ethnic backgrounds are also much more diverse today, with 44 per cent of Australians either having been born overseas or having at least one parent born overseas. Whereas those born overseas were almost all from Britain or Ireland when Donald Horne wrote his book, the mix is now much more diverse. The largest groups of migrants in Australia are still those from the UK, Ireland and New Zealand, but the balance of the migration has changed dramatically in recent years, with many more people arriving from China and the Indian sub-continent.

Food culture

As we have become a more affluent society, our patterns of consumption and behaviour have changed. In 1964 eating out was comparatively rare, with most families having a home-cooked meal together. There were no takeaway food outlets, although you could buy a hamburger or a milkshake at a local milk bar. The standard evening meal consisted of some meat and two or three vegetables. Following a 1954 referendum in New South Wales, pubs were able to stay open until 10 pm. Previously they had been required to close at 6 pm, leading to the extraordinary practice known as the 'six o'clock swill' – men crowding into bars after work to drink as much as they could in the short period before closing time. The change to the law was hotly contested, with the churches openly campaigning against the liberalisation of alcohol availability, and the vote was very close.

Small coffee shops were just starting to appear in Melbourne and Sydney, but it was not possible to get a decent cup of coffee in smaller towns until 20 or 30 years later. It was still illegal to have wine or beer with a meal outdoors when I moved to Brisbane; that only changed with the 1988 World Expo. The variety of food outlets we have today in our cities would have astonished Donald Horne. In 1964 there were a few Chinese restaurants, a very small number of Italian and Greek eateries, and not much else. Drinking wine was seen as peculiar behaviour, vegetarianism was almost unheard of and there were certainly no gluten-free options on the menu. The range of domestic appliances has also increased dramatically. In 1964 most kitchens had a stove and an ice-box or perhaps one of the new-fangled refrigerators, with a Mixmaster or similar device for doing the hard work of mixing batter or dough. We are now accustomed to having a wide range of labour-saving devices, bread-makers and coffee machines, blenders and grinders, sandwich-makers and microwave ovens, electric jugs and toasters, dishwashers and washing machines. Since our current level of material consumption is not sustainable, becoming a genuinely lucky country will require scaling back our material demands. The challenge is to do that while meeting the living standards we have come to expect.

Changes for women
As could have been predicted by anyone who thought about it, freeing women from the tyranny of child-bearing had huge social consequences. When the average woman married at 21 and had four or five children, most spent the next few decades largely engaged in domestic work which was certainly unpaid and often unvalued. The availability of safe and reliable contraception has allowed women to have broadly similar work and career opportunities to men. When Donald Horne wrote his book, there were very few female politicians, whereas women

have now been premiers in five of the six states, a prime minister and a governor-general. The only female sporting events that received any media coverage in 1964 were swimming, athletics and tennis; by contrast, as I was writing this chapter, I watched the trans-Tasman netball final and the Matildas playing in the soccer World Cup. Just before I began studying at the institution which became the University of New South Wales a few years later, the vice-chancellor lamented the fact that there were only seven women among its 7,000 students. While I was a student, that university educated Australia's first ever women graduates in Metallurgy and Chemical Engineering. Today, women are still less than 20 per cent of students in engineering, but overall there are more female undergraduates than male in the Australian university system.

When *The Lucky Country* was written, women teachers were expected to leave their jobs if they married; today, the majority of schoolteachers are women. At that time, doctors were male and nurses were female; today, both professions have roughly equal numbers of men and women entering those careers. There is still a significant level of discrimination against women, or at least an historic disadvantage that has not yet been overcome. In universities, the percentage of staff who are women systematically declines as you move up the hierarchy, with significantly fewer female professors than you would expect from the number of lecturers. In similar terms, Julia Gillard as prime minister was viciously attacked by opponents and media shock-jocks in ways that have never applied to men in the same position. She was alleged to have stabbed her predecessor in the back to become prime minister and have made an undertaking before the 2010 election that she failed to keep in office. The same comments could obviously be made about Tony Abbott, who rolled Malcolm Turnbull as leader of the Liberal Party and made a series of 2013 pre-election commitments he clearly had no intention of keeping, since some of them were mutually exclusive. He promised to reduce debt while abolishing two taxes and bringing in no new taxes, at the same time promising no cuts to health or education, no changes to pensions, and implementation of the extra government funding required for the Gonski reforms. For that matter, as mentioned earlier, Paul Keating became prime minister by displacing his elected leader, but the media did not make the sort of disparaging remarks about him that they made about Julia Gillard. While women are now as prominent as interviewers on TV current affairs programs as men, there are complaints when women like Leigh Sales or Emma Alberici are as assertive as men like Kerry O'Brien or Tony Jones. And studies show clearly that women still do the lion's share of work in the home, whether they are in the paid workforce or not. We still do not have anything like genuine equality of opportunity, even though the inequality has reduced dramatically in the last 50 years. I said 15 years ago that we will know we really have equality of opportunity when there are as many demonstrably incompetent women as men in senior jobs or in public office. That joke resonates because, as I wrote then, 'almost everyone can think of an incompetent man in a senior position, but women generally only reach such levels if they are extremely competent'.

TELLING OUR OWN STORIES

Maintaining our cultural attributes and social traditions depends critically on maintaining the capacity to tell our own stories in our own languages. That capacity has been steadily undermined by the failure of successive governments to maintain our cultural institutions. As Horne expressed it, 'we must have our own books about our own history and our own society, we must have our own fiction, our own poetry, our own plays, films, television series and also our own soap operas, our own social and political analysis, our own music and dance'. He went on to write, 'If we do not place cultural concerns at the centre of the contemplation and determination of our collective future, any political, social and economic attainments will be hollow, and our collective future bleak and meaningless.' The gradual colonisation of our media by the USA has significantly reduced both our capacity to tell our own stories and, arguably as a direct consequence, the level of public awareness of Australia's unique social history.

Whereas our arts were stimulated by governments after Donald Horne wrote, with both the Gorton Coalition government and the Whitlam ALP government supporting our film industry, more recent administrations have backed away from this policy. We are still seen as a good country in which to make movies, but the industry is now much more likely to make American films here than to tell our own stories in our own way. The 2005 Free Trade Agreement (FTA) with the USA diluted the legal requirements setting minimum levels of local content in commercial media like TV. Since it costs much less for a TV network to buy a series already produced for the US market than to produce serious local content, imported material has come to completely dominate Australian TV screens. The only significant exception is the spread of low-budget examples of 'reality TV' – surely the ultimate oxymoron, as there are few examples of entertainment that are further from reality.

The 2015–16 budget saw a massive cut to arts funding through the Australia Council. That body's funding allocation was effectively halved to allow the Commonwealth minister to hand out money to groups he approves of. Our two national television networks, the ABC and SBS, have both had their budgets slashed, despite pre-election promises by Tony Abbott that this would not happen. SBS has been forced to take advertisements, with the inevitable result that its programming has become blander so as not to offend its potential commercial interests. The ABC has been subjected to repeated attacks for being independent and not slavishly supporting the current government. These attacks have predictably had the effect of making the organisation less likely to air material that could be seen as critical of the government or its commercial supporters; in July 2015, it screened an almost embarrassing TV hagiography of Gina Rinehart, whose inherited wealth has made her Australia's richest woman. The Abbott government was outraged when the program *Q&A* included in its audience a Muslim activist, even though he was respectable enough to have been a paid columnist for the Murdoch press, saying that the *Q&A* audience was 'a lefty lynch mob' and banning Cabinet ministers from appearing on the program. In the absence of Barnaby Joyce, who had been booked to appear on the following program, the panel still included two representatives of the far right, one a regular columnist for *The Australian* and one from the Centre for Independent Studies. My assessment is that the ABC actually bends over backwards to accommodate right-wing views on *Q&A* because there are usually one or two panellists from that part of the political spectrum, but the Abbott government seemed unhappy that it wasn't supported by the entire line-up.

Donald Horne specifically argued that we would need to have the capacity to tell our own stories in our own language. The steady and systematic erosion of that critical capacity in recent decades was dramatically accelerated by the attacks on public broadcasting after the 2013 election of the Coalition government. Those attacks were predictably supported by the

Murdoch press, who would obviously prefer their view of the world not to be contrasted with that of public broadcasters like the ABC or SBS.

That being said, Australia has continued to make an impact in the developed world that is out of proportion to our population. Actors like Cate Blanchett, Geoffrey Rush, Guy Pearce, Nicole Kidman, Russell Crowe and Jacki Weaver are international stars. Entertainers like Barry Humphries and critics like Clive James are in great demand in the northern hemisphere. Golfers like Greg Norman and Adam Scott, footballers like Tim Cahill, tennis players like Pat Rafter and Lleyton Hewitt, swimmers like Ian Thorpe and Grant Hackett, cyclists like Cadel Evans, and cricketers like Shane Warne and Ricky Ponting are household names. Australia had a period of total domination of world cricket; and even soccer, long the Cinderella football code, emerged with the Socceroos qualifying for successive World Cups.

Our sporting success seems to have blinded us to the other problems discussed in this book. One critic described Australia as an 'inverse Achilles' – where the legendary hero's amazing strength was undone by the fatal weakness of one heel, Australia's overall weakness was obscured by our well-plated heel which deflected tiny arrows at Lord's cricket ground, on the lawn tennis courts of Wimbledon and the greens of St Andrew's golf course, on the roads of the Tour de France, in the Olympic pool and on the basketball court. Politicians have naturally fought for photo opportunities with sporting heroes. Following the tradition which has existed from Roman times of giving the masses bread and circuses, huge amounts of public money keep being found to construct or enhance football and cricket grounds, while millions are spent each year by successive Victorian governments subsidising an annual car race.

The Queensland government, struggling to find the money to provide education and health care services, could nevertheless guarantee hundreds of millions of dollars for facilities that will allow the Gold Coast to host the 2018 Commonwealth Games. Many South Australians were outraged when a state government that was cutting back on vital services like education and health care could find millions to upgrade the Adelaide Oval and build a huge footbridge to help spectators get there from the city centre. There is a popular belief that our governments will always be returned as long as there is cold beer in the fridge and some form of sport on television!

ALTERNATIVE FUTURES FOR DISCUSSION

We have a lot to discuss when considering what kind of Australia we want to be. To guide that discussion, various reports have set out the alternative futures for human society, facing the interconnected challenges of population growth, limited critical resources, constrained food production and serious environmental threats.

I discussed earlier the United Nations Environment Program (UNEP) reports on the *Global Environmental Outlook*. *GEO3*, released in 2002, sketched out four alternative possible responses to the emerging evidence of a global crisis. One they called 'Markets First' – increasing acceptance of expectations and values of the industrial world, trusting further globalisation and liberalisation of markets to enhance wealth and well-being. In this scenario, the attempts by ethical investors or consumer groups to exercise a corrective influence is 'undermined by economic imperatives' and the power of officials to protect social and environmental values is 'overwhelmed by expanding demands'. That is a grim but familiar future.

A more hopeful scenario is one that UNEP called 'Policy First' in which governments take decisive action to 'reach specific social and environmental goals', with environmental and social costs explicitly taken into account. This approach is certainly a better one in principle; the practical concern is whether the political will exists to take such an approach.

A more depressing prospect is what UNEP called 'Security First' – a world of increasing inequality in which the relatively well-off focus on protecting their islands of advantage by military force, leading inevitably to further inequality and likely serious conflict, if not the breakdown of civilised order as desperate people clamour to get into the enclaves of relative affluence. The accelerating flood of refugees into Europe is an indicator of what could happen if the disparity in material living conditions continues. While a significant number are fleeing the civil war in Syria, many of those arriving in rubber dinghies on Greek islands or the Italian coast are essentially economic refugees from other parts of the Middle East, African countries or the Indian sub-continent. As long as there are huge disparities in wealth between those areas and Europe, between Latin America and north America, between the Asia–Pacific region and Australia, the mass movement of people seeking a better life will continue.

The final and most optimistic scenario discussed by UNEP was 'Sustainability First':

> A new environment and development paradigm emerges in response to the challenge of sustainability, supported by new, more equitable, values and institutions. A more visionary state of affairs prevails, where radical shifts in the way people interact with one another and with the world around them stimulate and support sustainable policy measures and accountable

corporate behaviour. There is a much fuller collaboration between governments, citizens and other stakeholder groups in decision-making on issues of close common concern. A consensus is reached on what needs to be done to satisfy basic needs and realise personal goals without beggaring others or spoiling the outlook for posterity.

This most promising scenario presently seems the least probable. The Greek financial crisis appeared to underline the extent to which European leaders were driven by short-term economic priorities, determined to impose what they saw as fiscal discipline on Greece. This approach ignored the lessons of their own history. Most experts agree that the harsh terms imposed on Germany after World War I by the Treaty of Versailles caused the poverty and desperation of the Weimar Republic. That led directly to the rise of Hitler and the Nazi movement, which engulfed Europe in the unbelievable misery of World War II. The Allies learned this lesson and the agreement of 1945 did not impose similarly harsh conditions, allowing for the postwar reconstruction of Germany and the comparatively peaceful 70 years that has followed. There is a real fear that imposing harsh conditions on Greece will further increase inequality and fuel extremism. The former Greek finance minister Yanis Varoufakis told the ABC's Phillip Adams that the bail-out deal forced on Greece was 'a new Versailles Treaty'. Certainly such conditions are a long way from what UNEP called 'a new environment and development paradigm'.

Other voices are supporting the positive alternative of a societal transformation. In 2006, Brisbane hosted Earth Dialogues, a world forum for resource management and sustainable development. It was jointly chaired by Mikhail Gorbachev, former president of the Soviet Union and head of Green Cross

International, and Peter Beattie, then the Queensland premier. The theme of the meeting was that the front line of the battle for a truly peaceful world needed to be seen as sustainable development, respecting all people and the environment both now and for the future, with a priority of eradicating poverty. It went on to promote the Earth Charter as 'the ethical framework' for addressing the challenges we face, arguing that the charter's 'universal human values – respect, care, integrity and non-violence – transcend cultural differences' and should serve as our guides to a just and peaceful future. The Earth Charter had been launched at The Hague in 2000. It is 'a declaration of the fundamental principles for building a just, sustainable and peaceful global society in the 21st century'. It sets out those principles under four broad headings: 1. respect and care for the community of life; 2. ecological integrity; 3. social and economic justice; and 4. democracy, non-violence and peace. The summary document expresses the hope that ours will be a time 'remembered for the awakening of a new reverence for life, the firm resolve to achieve sustainability, the quickening of the struggle for justice and peace, and the joyful celebration of life'. While that is a laudable goal, it is difficult to reconcile with the world news we see every evening on our television screens.

The Great Transition Initiative

A group at the Tellus Institute in Boston, led by Dr Paul Raskin, has been the base for a program called the Great Transition Initiative (GTI), which has developed six future scenarios. The first two 'conventional worlds' either rely heavily on the self-correcting logic of competitive markets and tecYological innovation to reconcile growth with ecological limits (Market Forces); or rely on governments to push through incremental policy changes to slowly align the economy with the environment

(Policy Reform). The 'barbarisation' scenarios are Fortress Worlds, in which powerful international forces impose order by protecting elites in enclaves and locking out the impoverished majority; and Breakdown, which descends into chaos when environmental and social crises spiral out of control. Finally, the two 'great transition' scenarios are Eco-communalism, which returns to fiercely local communities on a small-scale, possibly as a recovery from a global disaster; and the New Sustainability Paradigm, which creates new 'categories of consciousness', with global rather than national citizenship sitting alongside democratic institutions of global governance.

Raskin developed his ideas further in an essay, *The Great Transition Today: A Report from the Future*, arguing that while the values that have driven human development for the last century – individualism, consumerism and domination of nature – have enabled very significant improvements in material well-being, they are now obstacles to a sustainable future. Raskin argues for 'a new triad' of values with ecological integrity replacing the domination of nature, individualism giving way to a sense of human solidarity, and the quality of the human experience replacing consumption. He sees those values as being applied in different ways and with different emphases in different societies, but argues that only that sort of transformation of values will allow a peaceful transition to a future that could be sustainable.

Reflecting on this analysis, it is very difficult to be optimistic about our future. We are currently trying the Market Forces approach, but the resulting environmental and social stresses appear unlikely to be corrected by the markets; if anything, the liberalisation of markets and the globalisation of the economy have accelerated environmental degradation and widened social inequality. Policy Reform has been limited to minor incremental advances and there is no obvious sign of the political will for the fundamental changes needed to shift the trajectory of development onto a path that would be sustainable. The world is becoming more divided between an affluent minority, literally making themselves unhealthy by the scale and nature of their consumption, and a majority still living in abject poverty. There is a real risk, as has been shown by a variety of studies ranging from *The Limits to Growth* in 1972 to *Food System Shock* in 2015, that the critical support systems for a civilised life could collapse, resulting in Fortress Worlds or Breakdown. If we are to have any chance of creating a New Sustainability Paradigm, we need to be taking action now.

WHAT CAN WE DO?

If we had leaders who were aware of events in the world and the large-scale global trends, they would be asking some obvious questions. What are the various probable futures for the world? How will Australia be affected? How are we positioned to take advantage of possible changes? Rational planning would try to position Australia for whichever of the possible futures does eventuate, rather than putting all of our national eggs in one basket, especially the fragile one of an assumed business-as-usual future. A positive approach would be to go further and try to influence which of the possible futures will eventuate, rather than standing passively on the global sidelines watching world events unfold. As a middle-rank power, the twelfth-largest economy in the world and currently a major commodity exporter, as well as having been (at least until recently) a respected contributor to UN agencies, Australia still has a great capacity to shape the global future.

In facing uncertain futures, Australia has a series of real advantages. We are one of only five OECD countries that have sufficient resources to meet the needs of our community; only New Zealand, Norway, Iceland and Canada share that good fortune. We are essentially self-sufficient in food, so we will be able to meet our needs if the global food trade networks fail. As an island nation, we have relatively little fear of border disputes. Despite the neglect of the last 25 years, we still have a strong base of scientific knowledge and capacity for innovation. One of the best legacies from our British colonial heritage is our strong social institutions. We have the general qualities set out in Donald Horne's list quoted earlier, all of which arguably equip us well for the uncertain futures we face.

At the personal level, there are simple steps we can all take, regardless of how responsible we have been in the past. We can all reduce our ecological footprint. We can all think more about the impacts of our choices on our fellow Australians. We can all do more to work with others for a better future. In *A Big Fix: Radical Solutions for Australia's Environmental Crisis* I suggested some practical things we can all do: use more-efficient appliances and use them less, go without meat at least one day a week, buy locally produced food, make our journeys shorter, walk or cycle or use public transport whenever we can. The global problems of resource depletion and environmental degradation are the sum of all the little choices we all make.

While there are many things we can do as individuals, our choices are limited by the broader social framework around us. We can't use public transport if it isn't frequent, reliable and safe. We can't buy local produce if it isn't on the shelves of our local shop. So we need our elected politicians to take the structural decisions that allow us to make responsible choices. That in turn means we need to act as responsible citizens and put pressure on our leaders to act in our long-term interests. Unless we urge elected representatives to adopt policies that are consistent with a sustainable Australia, we can't be surprised when they respond to the other pressures on them and continue to champion population growth, or lower taxes, or economic growth as the highest priority that overrides social cohesion and environmental protection.

A positive step could look like the one adopted by Rod Welford when he was Queensland Minister for Education, taking up a key recommendation from a working group that I chaired. He said that all schools should not just teach the basic principles of sustainability as part of the core curriculum, so all our young people will be equipped to make wise decisions, but also enact practical measures that reflect those principles in their use of paper, energy, other resources, water and so on. Futurist Dr Patricia Kelly has taken this argument a step further and argued that we should move beyond seeing ourselves as *Homo sapiens*, a term which is both gendered and a link to our evolutionary past, and see the goal of education as developing what she has called *Globo sapiens*: wise global citizens who are aware of the implications of their decisions and actions, willing and able to take responsibility for themselves, their communities and the planet.

In talking to politicians about the practical steps we need to take, I am often told that we can't afford to do what I suggest. But we also can't afford *not* to act responsibly, as we will pay a heavy price in the future if we don't prepare now for the sorts of shocks that are likely. At a more mundane level, I remind them that saying we can't afford something is not an absolute statement but a reflection of priorities. It is like me telling a group of students that I can't afford to take them to the pub for a drink at the end of a lecture. I am not saying that I would be bankrupt if I bought beer for 40 thirsty students; I am saying that I have better things to do with my money. When a government says it can't afford to do something you propose, they are effectively saying that it would be a lower priority than every one of the things that it does spend money on. That includes the multi-billion-dollar subsidies of fossil fuel supply and use, generous tax concessions for international corporations and superannuation schemes of wealthy individuals, negative gearing to encourage speculation in property, their own salaries and travel entitlements. It is easy to make a case for a responsible investment in our future being a higher priority than much of the current public expenditure, without even broaching the question of whether we should possibly pay more tax now to ensure that future generations can live as well as we do. We need to live more simply so that others can simply live – and we need to start that public discussion before it's too late.

ECONOMY

The processes of invention and innovation that are such an essential part of the Western Mind play a less domestic part in Australia than in any other prosperous country, apart from Canada. No matter what miracles Australians achieved in the earlier settlement of the continent and however spectacularly successful they can be at improvising when pushed to it, Australian businessmen [sic] have not proved to be very good at getting people to think up new things to make ... Unlike Sweden and Switzerland, Australia has not developed any significant specialties of its own in manufacture ...

Most of the manufacturing in what could accurately be described in the cliché term as a 'land rich in resources' is now under foreign control. The only major manufacturing industry groups that are not dominated by overseas firms are steel, cement, glass, sugar and paper. Of the top 100 Australian firms at least two-thirds are overseas-controlled ... The success of Australian industry in most significant sectors has been that of an advanced colonial society, with overseas capital and enterprise employing intelligent native labour [sic].
        —The Lucky Country, fifth edition, pp. 133–4

What Donald Horne wrote about the Australian economy 50 years ago is even more obviously true today. At the time he wrote, he could say that 'coal, steel and sugar' were our three biggest sectors of production and all were 'mostly owned locally'. The coal industry is now dominated by overseas firms and the steel industry has almost closed down. So Horne's warning of the need for new economic priorities, especially that of investing in science and research, still holds. Our economic direction since Horne's time, shifting away from Keynesian public investment to a market-reliant private sector, has shown a complete disregard for supporting innovation, whether through higher education, research opportunities or in the workforce itself. When this is combined with the pressures of an ever more global economy operating under a 'free trade' delusion, it means Australia will be very vulnerable economically in any crisis. It is possible, however, to see alternative futures in which we are much more self-reliant, have moved beyond the need for economic growth and prioritise the values of human well-being and happiness.

ECONOMIC POLICY

Keynesian public investment

When Horne was writing, most decision-makers accepted the prevailing economic ideas of Joÿ Maynard Keynes.

He responded to the Great Depression of the late 1920s and early 1930s by urging governments to spend on public infrastructure, thus employing people so they had money in their pockets and could buy the goods and services offered by the private sector. This approach had been broadly successful, although some economists have argued that the real recovery in the English-speaking world happened only when World War II caused a much greater increase in public spending. After the war ended, governments continued to pump public funds into large-scale projects. Probably the most important in Australia was the Snowy Mountains scheme, a massive undertaking to provide hydro-electricity to New South Wales and Victoria as well as irrigation water, by damming the Snowy River and sending water inland via huge turbines. At its peak the project employed several thousand people. To this day, about 10 per cent of the grid electricity used in the eastern states still comes from this huge development. Although Australia was governed from 1949 until 1972 by coalitions dominated by the Liberal Party, there was a national consensus that the government had a vital role in funding the essential infrastructure: roads, railways, airports, water supply, sewerage systems and so on. So public funds were continually used for projects in those areas, employing workers who were then able to spend their money on the goods and services offered by private sector companies.

Governments also funded public education systems of primary and secondary schools, based on the principles articulated by Henry Parkes at the time of federation: free, compulsory and secular education. There had historically been two groups of private schools, a large system operated by the Catholic Church and a small number of independent schools charging high fees, most obviously the so-called Great Public Schools. In the 1960s there was a vigorous debate about whether public funds should be provided to private schools. The debate was sparked by a recognition that many church schools were substandard in providing basic facilities like libraries and science laboratories. The major political parties started bidding for the votes of parishioners by promising 'state aid' for these schools, initially funds targeted to provide identified facilities like science labs. In more recent years, this bidding war has escalated into a broader diversion of public funds to private schools; under John Howard as prime minister, some of the richest private schools in the country were receiving large amounts of public funding while many state schools were struggling. The Rudd–Gillard–Rudd years saw accumulating concern about the problem lead to the Gonski report. Chaired by successful businessman, David Gonski, the Gonski inquiry showed that the funding disparity between schools was entrenching disadvantage and restricting opportunities for children in areas where the schools were poorly resourced. The government adopted the Gonski report and promised to improve the equality of opportunity by a staged reallocation of resources to poorer schools. The initiative was embraced by the state ALP governments of the time and also by the Coalition government in New South Wales. Before the 2013 election, the federal Coalition said it was equally committed to the Gonski reforms but, like some other pre-election commitments, the promise appears to have been only a device to attract swinging voters to its side. The national government has even been criticised by the NSW Coalition government for failing to implement the Gonski reforms. Investing in equality of educational opportunity is critical for our future.

The oil crisis

The broad commitment to public funding of infrastructure continued with the election in 1972 of the Whitlam government.

It had an ambitious program of investment in urban development, even creating the Department of Urban and Regional Development to oversee those plans. Like most other governments around the affluent world, the Whitlam government was then hit by a serious global economic problem arising from the so-called oil crisis. As discussed earlier, between 1972 and 1979, the world oil price increased from less than $2 to nearly $30 a barrel.

This had a huge economic effect because all the goods we use require petroleum fuels for their production and distribution. Developed economies experienced what was called 'stagflation' – a period in which prices rose rapidly but there was little or no economic growth. This meant that consumers experienced a lowering of their standard of living because prices were increasing, but the money they were earning was not. I remember vividly my personal experience of this effect. I had commenced lecturing at the UK Open University and had agreed to buy a small house. When I negotiated the loan to buy the property, the interest rate I was quoted was 4.5 per cent. As I signed the agreement, the rate had gone up to 5.5 per cent. When I made the first payment, the rate was 6.5 per cent. Within a year, it was 12.5 per cent. Simple arithmetic meant that the loan repayments, which were about one-third of my after-tax income when I agreed to take out the loan, had inflated to virtually my entire income! Only the generosity of the bank saved me from being evicted with my young family. My experience was repeated all around the affluent world.

The Whitlam government was very inexperienced, as the ALP had been in opposition for 23 years, and made several unwise decisions, but it was swimming against a very strong international economic tide. The 1975 election was complicated by the arguably unconstitutional action of the governor-general, JoŸ Kerr, when he removed the prime minister from office and installed the opposition leader, Malcolm Fraser, whose Liberal Party colleagues had been taking unprecedented action by blocking the government's money supply in the Senate. The public outrage at Kerr's action did not save the Whitlam government, which the electorate blamed for the declining economic situation. I was still in the UK in the late 1970s and saw the Labour government of Jim Callaghan suffer the same fate, leading to the election in 1979 of a Conservative government headed by Margaret Thatcher, just a few months before Ronald Reagan replaced Jimmy Carter as US president. In both cases, the old regime was voted out because it was judged, rightly or wrongly, responsible for the economic problems the countries suffered from the inflation of oil prices.

Reverting to market economies

Thatcher and Reagan came to office determined to overthrow the existing economic order. They had been influenced by a group of economists based in Chicago, the most prominent of whom was Milton Friedman. Friedman argued that the problems of the 1970s could be solved only by reversing the Keynesian policies. He urged governments to cut taxes – reducing the public provision of services – to 'make room' for the private sector. The Fraser government, with JoŸ Howard as its treasurer, started hesitantly down that path. The approach produced industrial conflict which was exploited by the ALP in the 1983 election, which brought Bob Hawke to power. But Hawke's formal education had been in economics, so he was sympathetic to the advice he and his treasurer, Paul Keating, were getting from Treasury, which had enthusiastically embraced the Chicago school's agenda of deregulation.

Under Hawke and Keating the Australian dollar was floated instead of having a fixed exchange rate, leading to the current situation in which we are told every night on the news what the dollar is worth against the euro, the British pound, the US dollar, the Japanese yen and so on, as if we should all be fixated on the games played by currency traders. Tariffs were reduced, on the grounds that this would force local producers to lift their game or lose their share of the local market. Of course, the inevitable result of this policy was that local manufacturers of labour-intensive products like clothing and footwear could not compete with producers in China, Vietnam, Thailand or the Philippines, where workers are paid a small fraction of Australian wages. It was equally inevitable that local manufacturers of high-technology products like consumer electronics and motor vehicles would find it difficult to compete with Japanese manufacturers, who benefit from larger domestic markets as well as a much greater level of support from their government. The run-down of Australian manufacturing, and the disappearance of tens of thousands of jobs in that field, was a direct and entirely predictable consequence of the reversion to the pre-Keynesian economic theories.

The level of government spending was a critical question affecting the 1993 election. Paul Keating had replaced Bob Hawke as the ALP prime minister after a party-room vote. John Hewson was the leader of the Liberal Party at the time and campaigned for election with his aggressive neoliberal economic agenda called Fightback! As discussed earlier, the re-election of Keating was seen as a public rejection of this extreme approach. John Howard was elected three years later, successfully harnessing growing public discontent with the Keating government. Under Howard, Australia's economic policy predictably moved further to the right, with a systematic run-down of public provision of essential services and associated reduction of taxes. Some of the reduction in Commonwealth taxes was offset by the introduction in 2000 of the Goods and Services Tax (GST). The GST was widely seen as a regressive measure, transferring more of the tax burden to lower income households, since it is calculated on the value of spending, whereas the income tax system is more generous to those on lower incomes. The same could be said of a range of recent policies such as negative gearing of investment properties and generous provisions for high-income superannuation. The decision of the Abbott government to abandon funding public transport in favour of urban road schemes could be interpreted as class warfare, since public transport is used much more by those on lower incomes. The Coalition government is also putting pressure on state governments to sell more of their public assets; in 2015, Joe Hockey as the treasurer told the newly elected Queensland government that they would not be given Commonwealth funding for infrastructure unless they sold some of their assets. The political problem was that the Queensland government had made a specific pre-election promise not to sell those assets. There was a similar situation in Victoria, where the ALP said before the 2015 election that they would cancel the East–West Link road proposed by the previous Coalition government. Having been elected on that promise and put forward proposals to use the funds much more effectively on public transport improvements, the Andrews government was urged by Tony Abbott to break their undertaking and reinstate the road project.

Ignoring well-being and happiness

Adam Smith is widely seen as the founder of the academic discipline of economics. His famous 1776 book *An Inquiry into the Nature and Causes of the Wealth of Nations* is best known for the celebration of self-interest in chapter 2. Smith argued that we do not get our dinner through the benevolence of the baker, the butcher and the brewer. When each follows their self-interest, he asserted, they are guided as if by an invisible hand to act in ways that are good for the community as a whole. This view that the community as a whole benefits when each of us follows our self-interest is the ideological basis of the Chicago school of economics. Its adherents seem unaware of the other ideas explored by Smith in this seminal book.

Although his writing essentially provided the foundations for the discipline of economics, Smith was a professor of moral philosophy. He was actually interested in the way economic transactions affected material well-being, rather than having the peculiar view that the market has an independent existence that needs to be recognised. Smith stressed the importance of the social fabric and the rule of law, pointing out that no financier would lend money and no employee would work unless they were confident that agreements would be honoured to repay loans or pay wages. He observed that markets only work properly if they are regulated by government to ensure there is no malpractice. Merchants will always be tempted to collude to raise prices and hold down wages, so governments need to ensure that price-fixing does not occur. In the eighteenth century, trade unions did not exist and it was illegal for workers to combine to try to get fairer wages. Smith also saw that one provider could hold up prices and profiteer by having control of a critical tecŸology or by buying up competitors to achieve a monopoly, warning that it would be necessary for governments to prevent this happening if they were concerned about such abstract notions as fairness and efficiency. Fundamentally, he also saw that allowing market forces to reign would inevitably widen the gap between rich and poor, as those with more funds would always be able to invest profitably as well as being able to procure better nutrition, better sanitation, better health care and better education for their children. So he argued that governments had a responsibility to maintain the social order by restraining those negative forces with active policies to ensure a fairer (or, at least, less unfair) distribution of incomes and other assets.

None of those essential qualifications appears in the economic policies being followed in the English-speaking world since the overthrow of Keynesian economics. Andrew Leigh's recent book *Battlers and Billionaires* documents in great detail the consequences of the new economic approach. The disparity between rich and poor in Australia gradually narrowed between federation and the early 1970s. A succession of innovations such as the eight-hour day, the basic wage, medical insurance and the public provision of such essential services as education and transport had turned Australia into what Donald Horne saw as perhaps the most equal society that had ever existed. The statistics show he was right, but the situation began to change in 1975. Leigh quoted some figures to illustrate the change. Since 1975, full-time wages for the median employee have increased 35 per cent, after inflation. But those on low incomes have seen their wages rise only 15 per cent, while those on high incomes have received increases of nearly 60 per cent. Corporate executives have done much better. Just between 1993 and 2009, the average amounts paid to CEOs of our 100 largest companies rose from $1 million (17 times the average earnings) to $3 million (42 times the average earnings). By 2013, the top 20 CEOs were being paid more than 100 times the average wage. Change has accelerated since then, so that Australian society is now more unequal than it was 100 years ago. We have more very rich people and more people living below the poverty line than ever before.

The widening disparity of incomes is not the only cause of inequality. There has also been a steady erosion of the public provision of essential services like education, transport and health care in favour of a private-provider model. It means that those with heavier wallets have more choices than those with limited incomes. As Leigh pointed out, we now have areas with entrenched disadvantage. Low-income suburbs and rural regions tend to have poorer public schools, as Gonski reported. So the children in those areas are less likely to receive the education that will give them economic opportunities in the modern workforce. That in turn means they will have lower incomes, so they will live in poorer areas and their children will not have the education that will give *them* economic opportunities. This is a very strong feedback loop, locking the poorest people into an endless cycle of disadvantage. The Gonski reforms were intended to address this problem, but the Coalition government had shown no sign of being prepared to implement the proposed changes as I was writing this book.

Zombie economics

JoŸ Quiggin, professor of economics at the University of Queensland, has written about what he called 'zombie economics' – the undead ideas that still prowl around the political landscape. The first and most fundamental of these is the 'trickle-down effect' which argues that the whole community will benefit if governments encourage a small number of people to become wealthy, since they will spend their money in ways that benefit everybody. Quiggin refutes this idea, showing that there is no evidence anywhere in the world that the community as a whole benefits if a small group of people become very wealthy. They are much more likely, both in theory and as observed in practice, to engage in behaviour that brings no benefit to the rest of the community, such as bidding up the price of luxury items like lavish housing and 'trophy houses' in holiday areas.

Similarly, Ross Gittins, who is economics editor of *The Sydney Morning Herald*, argued in his book *The Happy Economist* that the whole economics profession has lost sight of its original goal, which was improving human welfare and increasing happiness. These are slippery concepts that are very hard to measure, as Gittins acknowledges. On the other hand, he says, the sum of economic activity by way of spending is easy to measure. So the total amount of economic activity, measured as the Gross Domestic Product (GDP), has become effectively the measure of progress. But it is fundamentally flawed as a measure – because it counts financial transactions only, it ignores significant areas of activity. If I cook a meal for a group of people, no money changes hands so there is no contribution to the GDP. If I had taken the same group of people to a local restaurant, there would have been a financial transaction that counted in the GDP. In similar terms, much of the domestic work that is done does not count, nor does most of the child care. It is clearly absurd that activities like cooking, cleaning and care of children seem important to our society only if they become commercial operations. Even worse, occurrences that lower our quality of life like accidents, crime and violence contribute to the GDP. If a vandal were to break the left headlight of every car in a car park, they would increase the GDP considerably. If they broke both headlights in every car, they would do twice as much to boost the economy, and if they were to smash every windscreen as well they would be a minor economic miracle! As Gittins says, the GDP does not measure some really important things, but does count some serious negatives. It is a poor measure of economic success.

Others have gone further in criticising the obsession with the GDP. The late US senator Robert Kennedy said in a speech in 1968, shortly before his campaign for the presidency was cut short by an assassin:

> Gross National Product counts air pollution and cigarette advertising, and ambulances to clear our highways of carnage. It counts special locks for our doors and the jails for the people who break them. It counts the destruction of the redwood and the loss of our natural wonder in chaotic sprawl. It counts napalm and counts nuclear warheads and armored cars for the police to fight the riots in our cities. It counts Whitman's rifle and Speck's knife, and the television programs which glorify violence in order to sell toys to our children.
>
> Yet the Gross National Product does not allow for the health of our children, the quality of their education or the joy of their play. It does not include the beauty of our poetry or the strength of our marriages, the intelligence of our public debate or the integrity of our public officials. It measures neither our wit nor our courage, neither our wisdom nor our learning, neither our compassion nor our devotion to our country, it measures everything in short, except that which makes life worthwhile.

It is worth noting that even thoughtful Liberal Party politicians have canvassed this difficult subject. When Dick Hamer, Liberal Premier of Victoria from 1972 to 1981, presented his first budget, he said that more and more people around the world were questioning 'the validity of material growth as an end in itself', especially if its pursuit meant 'the things of the spirit are dimmed and the very environment in which we live is threatened'. He asked whether politicians should be thinking of 'Gross National Wellbeing' rather than the Gross National Product, urging his colleagues to place 'a greater emphasis on the very essence of the quality and purpose of life'.

Contemporary critics of the obsession with economic growth are more trenchant. Writing in *The Guardian* in 2014, British social critic George Monbiot said:

> To try to stabilise the system, governments behave like soldiers billeted in an ancient manor who burn the furniture, the panelling, the paintings and the stairs to keep themselves warm for a night … breaking up our public health services, social safety nets and above all the living world, to produce ephemeral spurts of growth. Magnificent habitats, the benign and fragile climate in which we have prospered, species that have lived on Earth for millions of years, all are being stacked on the fire, their protection seen as an impediment to growth.
>
> Why are we wrecking the natural world and public services to generate growth, when that growth is not delivering contentment, security or even, for most of us, greater prosperity? Why have we enthroned growth, regardless of its utility, above all other outcomes? Why, despite failures … have we not changed the model?

The obsession with the GDP, as if it were a genuine measure of well-being, is a fundamental failing of modern economics. There have been serious proposals to replace it with a more relevant measure, such as the Genuine Progress Indicator (GPI), which essentially deducts from the GDP negative expenditures such as the cost of illness and crime, as well as defensive expenditure such as security measures to deter robberies. Probably the most important reason why governments resist the use of the GPI is that it shows that Australians are worse off now than they were 40 years ago! While the GPI is a more sensible measure than the GDP, it still fails to include the unpaid work done in the home, or in the community by volunteers. Lifesaving clubs, rural fire brigades, Meals-on-Wheels and similar organisations are largely staffed by volunteers, but make a huge contribution to our quality of life. Most people would agree that it is better for infants to be nurtured by a parent than for them to be in commercial child-care organisations, or to have healthy home-cooked meals rather than buying takeaway food, but the economic calculus completely reverses this priority.

As John Kenneth Galbraith wrote in *The New Industrial State* nearly 50 years ago, the development of complex societies has led to a situation in which politics has become seen as little more than economic management. Politicians and pundits alike so fully embrace this notion that they appear puzzled when governments are voted out despite economic prosperity, or are returned despite difficult economic times. In the real world, people vote for a particular political party for a range of reasons, most generally because they identify with the overall world view or ideology of that party. Its economic policy and its claim to successful economic management form only one aspect on which parties are judged; voters also think about their attitudes to education, health care, environmental protection, infrastructure development, planning and so on, as well as the appeal of their political representatives. As both Kerryn Higgs and John Quiggin have argued, we would be better off if decision-makers recognised the complexity of the real world and saw economic development as a way to improve human welfare, rather than as an end in itself. That would see a different approach to education.

HIGHER EDUCATION

Public investment in the common good
When I was young, full-time higher education was quite expensive and so it was restricted to those with wealthy parents or

those who were successful in competing for a Commonwealth Scholarship or Teachers College Scholarship which paid the fees. Even those avenues were really only open to those living in the city, or rural young people with parents who were able to help with the costs of living away from home. Until the mid-1950s there had been one university in each state, supplemented in the early 1960s by the new Australian National University in Canberra. Beginning in the mid-1950s, the new University of Tec̈yology in Sydney offered part-time courses in science, the applied sciences and engineering, but that was an innovation generally regarded with suspicion by the established universities. In 1961 that institution added Arts and Medicine to its offerings and became the University of New South Wales (UNSW). In the following years Monash University in Melbourne and Macquarie University in Sydney were established and some branches of older universities became autonomous institutions: University of New England had begun life as a college of the University of Sydney, Newcastle and Wollongong universities as colleges of UNSW, James Cook University as a college of the University of Queensland.

While the Liberal-led coalition under Robert Menzies had been essentially conservative, it did believe in the long-term benefits of investing in education. The 1956 Murray report led to a significant Commonwealth contribution to universities which had traditionally been institutions governed by state legislation and funded by state governments. That started a process of levelling-up salaries and conditions in states which historically had shown little interest in the funding of higher education, most conspicuously Tasmania and Queensland. But at the time Donald Horne was writing his book, still only about 5 per cent of Australian school leavers went on to higher education, so there were only about 70,000 students in the eight universities that existed.

There was a fundamental change when the Whitlam government was elected in 1972. As well as believing in the benefits to the community of investing in higher education, Whitlam believed in the increased benefits of making higher education available to all those who were capable of further study. So his government abolished university fees and increased funding to allow the expansion of universities. With the financial barrier removed, there was a dramatic increase in the number of school-leavers going on to higher education. Many of today's decision-makers reaped the benefit of this change; they were able to study full-time without paying fees. The teachers colleges had been set up to train those who would become schoolteachers. In the 1970s, some were expanded to become colleges of advanced education (CAEs), while new CAEs were created, providing courses in such areas as nursing and hotel management. Both universities and CAEs expanded through the 1970s. By the end of the Whitlam government in 1975 there were 17 universities and 77 CAEs with total enrolments of about 230,000 students: three times the number a decade earlier.

Reframing higher education as a private investment

Enrolments continued to increase into the 1980s, increasing the cost to the Commonwealth government. In 1988, under the Hawke government, education minister JoŸ Dawkins announced a fundamental and far-reaching change to education. Essentially he abolished the distinction between universities and CAEs, encouraged mergers to form larger units and renounced the commitment to supporting higher education without fees. There had already been significant changes since 1975; the Dawkins reforms converted the 19 universities and 54 CAEs into 39 universities. Some of these were the result of absorbing former CAEs into the previously existing universities.

In south-east Queensland the Agricultural College at Gatton became part of the University of Queensland, CAEs at Kelvin Grove and Carseldine became part of Queensland University of TecŸology, while CAEs at Mount Gravatt and the Gold Coast joined Griffith University, as did the Conservatorium of Music and the College of Art. While the mergers were claimed to improve the cost-effectiveness of higher education by producing economies of scale, in practice they added an extra layer of management in most institutions and added significant complexity by forcing very different cultures to combine into new multi-faceted organisations.

To soften the blow of reintroducing tuition fees, Dawkins introduced the Higher Education Contribution Scheme (HECS). It was an accurate title: students contribute to the cost of their education. They incur a debt while studying and are expected to repay that debt after graduating. While this was politically cunning in the short term and undoubtedly reduced the hostility that would otherwise have been caused by the reintroduction of fees, I believe it has had a catastrophic long-term effect. The Dawkins reforms reframed university education so that it was no longer seen as a public investment in the common good, but a private investment in future earning capacity. That in turn rapidly shifted enrolments away from areas of study that do not obviously translate into higher earnings, like classics, the humanities, mathematics, science and even some areas of engineering. It created a surge in enrolments for courses that are seen, rightly or wrongly, as a licence to print money: law, commerce, medicine, business studies. Where medicine had traditionally been studied by those who felt a vocation for that profession, there soon became intense competition for places in courses that were seen as giving high future incomes. The consequent entry into medical courses of high-achieving school leavers with little aptitude for the profession became a significant problem, leading to most universities scrapping the practice of allowing entry into medicine courses from school; most now have graduate-entry medical degrees and interview potential applicants to try to ascertain their true suitability for medical careers. The increase in the number of students studying law has resulted in there being far more law graduates than were needed. This has in turn created a whole network of ambulance-chasing law firms offering to sue somebody on your behalf if you suffered injury, real or imagined, leading to ridiculous situations where community activities have been made impractical by the escalating cost of insuring against legal action. It is a classic example of the adage that you can never change only one thing in a complex system; there are always flow-on effects.

The Hawke–Keating government also introduced the possibility of universities accepting full-fee-paying students from overseas. Predictably, once that happened there was obvious pressure to allow more local students into universities, even if they did not appear to meet academic entry standards, if they were prepared to pay the same fees. There is now evidence that the economic emphasis has corrupted the academic integrity of our universities. The ABCs *Four Corners* even aired a program in 2015 looking at the particular problem arising from the rapid expansion of overseas student numbers. Some courses are now so dependent on the fee income from overseas students that they literally cannot afford to fail the students, even if their work is substandard. There have been several recent instances of junior staff blowing the whistle about the lowering of standards to allow fee-paying students to continue or graduate; in every case, the university has cracked down on the whistleblower rather than addressing the root of the problem. I know of one instance where a senior academic was told that his contract would not be renewed because he refused to pressure staff to lower standards. From the perspective of the overseas students, some feel they are being charged high fees for courses taught mainly by casual staff on short-term contracts, so they aren't sure they are getting good value for their money. While the current approach deals with the short-term need to keep fee-paying students in the system and maintain the income levels needed to pay staff and service facilities, there is a real risk that the standing of Australian degrees (and their consequent ability to attract fee-paying students from overseas) will be eroded. When I graduated, an Australian honours degree was unquestioningly accepted by British universities as being of equivalent standard, whereas they had lists of the relatively small number of US universities that were seen as producing graduates able to move on to higher degree study in the UK. I foresee a situation where Australian institutions will be in that same category, with a selective approach to establishing which institutions produce graduates who meet international standards.

Negative effects on public debate

In 2014, the Abbott government decided to reduce still further the public funding of universities. They sought to soften the blow and recruit some university managers to their cause by proposing to allow the institutions greater freedom to set their fees. The implication was obvious. If the public funding of universities were to be further reduced, they would have to increase the charges to students to meet their income requirements. It was perhaps not surprising that most of the oldest and largest universities judged the proposal as being in their interest and supported the scheme. University staff and the community did not, and an effective campaign against the likelihood of '$100,000 degrees' persuaded the cross-bench senators not to endorse the government's agenda. After Malcolm Turnbull replaced Tony Abbott as prime minister, the government accepted that its 'deregulation' proposal was not going to be supported and formally withdrew it.

That has not solved the problem, however, which is that the government's ideological commitment to reducing public spending is running down the capacity of universities to offer quality education. This in turn has implications for staffing. Recent studies have shown that the majority of undergraduate teaching is now done by staff on casual contracts, many of whom do not know from one year to the next whether they will be re-employed. This saves the universities money, but it must have an effect on the quality of education if most of the teaching staff are as concerned about their continuing job security as they are about student learning. Many of those casual staff understandably feel the university has no loyalty to them, but their insecure employment means they dare not criticise.

The move toward casual staff has affected other functions of the universities. It is impossible to plan long-term research projects that challenge fundamental ideas if you don't have job security. Most casual staff are reluctant to engage in debate on important public issues, not just seeing that as a distraction from their core business but also being worried that it might prejudice their chances of continuing employment. Thirty years ago, I wrote a report about the tradition of academic tenure. This was the practice of giving academics the security to engage in debate on important public issues in their areas of expertise by protecting them from being dismissed for taking unconventional or unpopular stances. I argued that an important function of universities has been to act as the conscience and critic of society. When I came to Queensland in 1980, the only criticism of the corrupt Bjelke-Petersen government came from a small number of academics and an even smaller number of the clergy. The commercial media were silent and most business people knew the consequences of offending the government. With fewer of the academic staff now having secure employment, it is inevitable that fewer will feel free to contribute to public discussion on important issues. I believe that the community as a whole suffers if this contribution is reduced. The fact that most public discussion on important issues is at the trivial and superficial level cannot be attributed solely to the erosion of academic tenure and the consequent reluctance of experts to speak out fearlessly, but it certainly is a contributing factor.

Narrowing of student life

While the majority of students are nominally studying full-time, in practice most students now have to work to meet their living costs, inevitably reducing the time they have available to study. This is one aspect of the radical changes to the pattern of university education in the last 50 years. In 1964 when *The Lucky Country* was published, I was a part-time student at UNSW. Courses ran for the full academic year, from February to November, with assessment almost entirely based on end-of-year exams. There was some student discontent with this approach, basically because a whole year's work could be undone by illness at the critical time of the year, or even just by performing badly under pressure of examination conditions. So students in the 1960s campaigned for a revision to the assessment system, with some credit for work done during the course of the year.

While the old system disadvantaged some students, it suited others. The standing joke of the time was that in first term, new students worked, in second term nobody worked and in third term everybody worked. Like most standing jokes, it had an element of truth. It was true that students could ease off during the year and spend time on extracurricular activities, as long as they put in a big effort in the weeks leading up to the end-of-year exams. So drama, debating and inter-departmental sport flourished in the middle months of the year. That not only gave students a broader experience, but also had the desirable effect of forcing them to interact with people studying in totally different areas. In the drama society or on the rugby field, science students mixed with those studying arts, medicine, law or engineering, leading not just to permanent friendships but also to greater awareness of fields they were not systematically studying. My education in engineering and science certainly benefited from the interactions I had in extracurricular activities with students from other fields, especially the humanities and the social sciences.

Today universities have adopted a semester model and introduced systems of continuous assessment, so students have to submit items of work almost every week. It is a fairer system of assessing students' progress, but it has destroyed their capacity to engage in other activities. Some academics have also expressed concern that students can study small sections of the field one at a time and collect enough credit to pass a course, without ever having to demonstrate their ability to integrate those different elements. In fields such as engineering, architecture and medicine, it is a real concern if students can become qualified professionals without ever having to show they can put all these elements together in practice.

How higher education changes will hurt us

The higher education system of today takes in a much larger fraction of school-leavers than it did 50 years ago. That is consistent with a general trend in the affluent world. However, we still lag well behind many countries. In 2012, about 35 per cent of Australians between the ages of 25 and 64 had at least completed secondary school. The OECD average was 45 per cent, while leading countries like Japan, Sweden and Germany had figures above 50 per cent. That is a striking difference: just over a third of adult Australians had completed secondary school or done some tertiary education, compared with over half in the countries that are most competitive in the value-adding, knowledge-intensive industries of this century. The OECD classification of these industries includes high-technology manufactures such as aircraft, computers, communications equipment and pharmaceuticals, medium-technology manufactures such as motor vehicles and electrical machinery, as well as some knowledge-intensive service sectors like education, health care and financial services.

Australia has always educated relatively few engineers and scientists per head of population, compared with other advanced economies. The changes of recent years have widened the gap between those who could potentially produce new knowledge and those who might regulate it. We graduate far more lawyers each year than engineers, whereas the opposite is true of Japan. The young Australian of today is much more likely to finish secondary school and very much more likely to go on to higher education than when *The Lucky Country* was published, but the whole notion of higher education and workforce planning has been abandoned in favour of a market-oriented approach.

As an extreme example, when I was on the full-time staff of Griffith University, we introduced a small elective in forensic science. Because it is a subject that interests potential students, especially when there are several TV programs that illustrate the fascinating aspects of the profession, several universities now offer courses of this kind. So we are graduating each year more than a hundred people with advanced skills in forensic science, even though there is typically about one job vacancy a year in the entire country in that field. There has been serious criticism, in my view quite well-founded, of the willingness of universities to enrol and educate students in fields for which the job prospects are very limited. The science and technology academies have repeatedly expressed concern about our failure to attract talented young people to careers in maths, science and engineering. As long as careers in science and engineering look insecure and poorly paid compared with commerce, law and medicine, students will be driven by the current approach toward the fields that look more likely to allow them to recoup their large investment in a degree. This almost guarantees that we will not be competitive in the emerging industries of the twenty-first century.

SCIENCE

Fifty years ago, the Commonwealth Scientific and Industrial Research Organisation (CSIRO) was seen by governments as an outstanding Australian achievement. It was recognised internationally both for its scientific excellence and its ability to translate research findings into practical outcomes for the community. Originally established to support farming and grazing, it had gradually broadened its work to include the basic science of manufacturing, communications and food production. Australia also had other government science agencies. I spent three months working for the Defence Standards Laboratories (DSL) after doing my honours year in physics, working on a technique that allowed improved analysis of impurities in metals and alloys. The DSL's broad mission is to improve the scientific underpinning of the activities supporting our defence forces.

We also had an Australian Atomic Energy Commission (AAEC), chaired by the first vice-chancellor of UNSW, Sir Philip Baxter. At the time, the UK and the USA had devised ways of producing electricity from the tecÿology used to build the nuclear weapons that destroyed Hiroshima and Nagasaki. There was great enthusiasm for the potential of this new energy source, which promised to make obsolete the dangerous and dirty process of mining and burning coal to produce electricity. Most of the states were positive about the possibility of using nuclear energy and the AAEC had been established to provide the scientific expertise which would be needed. It was given approval and funding to build a research reactor at Lucas Heights, which at the time was in remote bushland well away from the suburbs of Sydney. I can remember scientists from the city car-pooling to attend a guest lecture there by a distinguished visiting physicist. UNSW ran courses in nuclear engineering to equip graduates with the skills which the new industry would demand. There was broad acceptance in 1964 that investing in science would give us all a brighter future.

Research funding

While science was seen as having provided the knowledge base which had dramatically improved our quality of life, it was still being done on the proverbial shoestring. University physicists led their graduate students on raids to municipal rubbish tips to find items that could be recycled into apparatus for their research: refrigerator motors and compressors, vacuum cleaners and pieces of disused plumbing were joyfully carried back to university laboratories. Glass-blowers and lens-grinders worked to fashion experimental equipment from cheap supplies. Life for the scientists gradually improved. When I returned to Australia in 1980, having done doctoral research in the UK and then worked in a university there for nine years, I joined the School of Science at the relatively new Griffith University. Its recurrent budget allowed it to provide each academic with a small annual allocation for basic research needs. It was necessary to apply to a granting agency for funds for more ambitious projects, but there was at least pump-priming money to allow researchers to establish their career and submit credible proposals for research grants. Success rates for proposals to the major research agencies like the Australian Research Council (ARC), the National Health and Medical Research Council (NHMRC) and the National Energy Research, Development and Demonstration Council were good enough to justify putting serious effort into writing grant applications. The successive annual reports in the 1980s showed that the majority of my science colleagues at Griffith University had support from one or more of the granting agencies.

With the significant expansion of the university system, neither the core funding of universities nor the budgets of research granting agencies have kept pace, so the success rates of grant applications are now a serious worry. The NHMRC in 2014 judged that about three-quarters of the proposals it received were of high enough quality to deserve funding, but they were able to support only 15 per cent of the applications. It is clearly a waste of productive talent if we encourage the best researchers to apply for competitive grants, subject the applications to serious peer review, then send 85 per cent of them away empty-handed. The situation is even worse for basic science, because the NHMRC budget for medical research has increased faster than the allocation to the ARC, while the separate energy research fund was abolished 20 years ago. Medical researchers also have a range of charitable foundations with resources to support research. The Australian Chief Scientist and other leading scientists, including our living Nobel Laureates, have publicly lamented the failure to provide funding and career opportunities to young scientists. Both are important; in 2015, we even saw a highly qualified Australian scientist working overseas decide to relinquish a prestigious three-year research fellowship in this country because of the scarcity of career opportunities at the end of that short period.

The introduction of HECS, discussed earlier, has also given our most talented science graduates a financial incentive to go overseas and stay there. By the time they have completed a bachelor's degree and a doctorate, they have piled up a huge debt which they have to repay if they take a professional job in Australia. If they go overseas, for example for a post-doctoral fellowship, they can live on their earnings rather than paying a significant fraction back to the government. Staying here, or coming back to their home country after a short period of overseas experience, involves a big financial sacrifice. Many do it for family reasons or as a lifestyle choice; I finally returned to Australia after completing a doctorate at a British university and working in the UK for many years, primarily because I wanted my children to grow up here. If we want to be a clever country, we should be encouraging our best and brightest to come back to Australia, rather than putting barriers in their way.

Science funding by the Australian government is now at its lowest in 30 years. CSIRO made hundreds of scientists redundant in response to the 2014–15 budget. For the first time in decades, we did not even have a Minister for Science. The title was subsequently added to the responsibilities of another minister, but science has certainly remained a low priority. Funding for CSIRO and the Defence Science and TecŸology Organisation was cut further in the 2015–16 budget. The government did provide modest increased funding for biomedical research, after an unsuccessful attempt to persuade the Senate to fund this investment by increasing the costs of GP visits.

The Australian government's suspicion of science reached a point of high farce in 2015 when the then chair of the Prime Minister's Business Advisory Council, Maurice Newman, made the astonishing claim that the world's climate scientists are part of a gigantic conspiracy, coordinated by the United Nations, to destroy democratic institutions and usher in a brave new world of global government. I observed at the time that this would be an even more improbable conspiracy than the claims that the moon landings had been faked on a Hollywood back lot. At least that would have only required collusion between an efficient technical body, the US National Aeronautics and Space Administration, and a small group of film professionals. It is literally incredible that the UN, which is hardly a watchword for smooth organisation, could be directing thousands of climate scientists around the world to fabricate evidence so convincingly that national science academies and elected governments have been persuaded to respond to a problem that doesn't exist. Perhaps more worrying even than this extraordinary statement by the prime minister's adviser, within a few days one of the government's elected members, South Australian senator Cory Bernardi, published a letter to the editor of the national daily newspaper, praising the adviser for his courageous intervention!

As another example of the anti-science approach of the Abbott government, several senior members attacked wind energy schemes and supported the urban myth that wind farms cause a range of insidious health effects. The government actually directed the NHMRC to fund research into these ailments, even though there is no solid evidence that wind farms have any impact on human health at the distances required by law from the nearest dwellings. Funds were also found to appoint a wind energy commissioner, a public official to receive complaints about alleged health problems, as if the Abbott government were actively sabotaging the industry. The 2015 change in the prime ministership has at least ended this bizarre chapter of anti-science public policy.

Research facilities

It has been clear for decades that Australia cannot be competitive in high-end research. The sort of fundamental atomic physics pursued by CERN (the European Organization for Nuclear Research) or the plasma research aimed at producing nuclear fusion, can be carried out only by international collaboration. In those special examples, there is literally only one experimental site for the entire global scientific community. More generally, as the cost of sophisticated equipment has risen beyond the reach of Australian scientists, we have seen an increasing tendency for 'suitcase science' – researchers packing their bags and going to the major international laboratories to carry out their experiments. Where Australia has always had an advantage is in areas of research that take advantage of our position, either the local biological or geological features or our position in the southern hemisphere providing opportunities in astronomy. Our access to parts of the sky not visible from the northern hemisphere has resulted in the reverse of suitcase science: astronomers from Europe and the USA come to use our optical and radio telescopes. The Anglo-Australian telescope at Siding Spring in New South Wales has become a major site for astronomical research, while Australia and South Africa have been jointly chosen for the most ambitious terrestrial telescope ever built, the so-called Square Kilometre Array.

There were serious proposals to build nuclear power stations in the 1960s, but these all failed the test of economic feasibility:

it was simply cheaper to build and operate coal-fired power stations. The last proposal to survive was for a power station on Commonwealth land at Jervis Bay, on the NSW south coast. That was finally cancelled by the Whitlam government in the early 1970s. Disgruntled employees of the AAEC or the UNSW Nuclear Engineering School kept agitating for a revival of nuclear power, but the issue held little political interest until the early twenty-first century. There was, however, growing recognition of the usefulness of radioactive substances in medicine, both for diagnostic purposes and cancer treatments. With nuclear energy no longer on the agenda, the AAEC was renamed the Australian Nuclear Science and TecŸology Organisation (ANSTO). While the research reactor at Lucas Heights continued to do fundamental research in physics, the 'nuclear science' part of the name, it also produced isotopes for nuclear medicine and a smaller quantity for industrial use. This became a major consideration when the reactor, built back in the 1950s, reached the end of its useful life at the turn of the century. There was a vigorous debate about whether it should be replaced. One view was that the main purpose of the facility was to provide the expertise for nuclear power, so there was no need to spend hundreds of millions on a replacement in the absence of any plan to build power reactors. The opposite view, which carried the day after a long argument, was that the reactor also produced radioactive materials for medical and industrial use; given the large and growing demand for these materials, there would be a need either for alternative production methods to be built or for large-scale imports of radioactive materials to be allowed. The Australian government eventually approved the construction of the OPAL reactor, which is now in operation at Lucas Heights.

A political problem is that this ANSTO site is no longer a large distance from the Sydney suburbs, which have sprawled to and around the reactor location. Although the reactor was there long before the suburbs, some of the residents are unhappy about the proximity of their houses to the ANSTO facility. Predictably, each of the major nuclear accidents overseas – Three Mile Island in 1979, Chernobyl in 1986 and Fukushima in 2011 – has provoked local community concern. The NSW government has responded to community concern by saying it is unhappy for radioactive waste to be stored at the ANSTO Lucas Heights site. In the absence of a secure national repository for the waste, temporary permission has been given for storage there of the waste that resulted from the decommissioned reactor. Since it is impractical either to relocate the reactor or reconfigure the Sydney suburbs, the existing situation will continue. The Commonwealth government has made several unsuccessful attempts to establish a national repository for radioactive waste. All have encountered local opposition. Another attempt was under way as I was writing this book, but the changes to ministerial responsibilities when Malcolm Turnbull took over as prime minister caused a delay in the process. There will probably be a public inquiry in 2016 into a proposed site.

Commercial innovation

While governments have systematically wound back our commitment to science and innovation in the last 25 years, we still have an enviable record. Science is an area in which Australia really does punch above our weight. One indicator is the number of Nobel Prizes in the sciences: physics, chemistry, biological sciences and medicine. Australia has more Nobel Laureates (13) than China (9), which has a much larger population and many more scientists. We should not be over-satisfied, however; New Zealand, with its much smaller population, has won as many Nobel Prizes as Australia, and Sweden has won about twice as many as we have. With about 0.3 per cent of the world population, we produce about 2 per cent of all scientific papers. Studies also show that Australian science is disproportionately influential; in other words, papers published by Australian scientists have an above-average chance of being cited by other researchers. Where we fall down, by international standards, is in translating our science into commercial products or community benefits. When I was director of the Science Policy Research Centre at Griffith University in the 1980s, it was clear that Australia's investment in basic research in CSIRO and universities was about par for OECD countries, but our private-sector research funding was only a fraction of the figure elsewhere, so we lagged badly in commercial innovation.

This problem was recognised in the late 1980s, when the government's Chief Scientist (Dr Ralph Slatyer) championed the development of Cooperative Research Centres. This was an imaginative response to an age-old problem. It has been said that trying to direct scientific researchers is like trying to herd cats! The extension of that metaphor is that you can make cats go where you want if you have a bowl of cream. Slatyer's vision was to provide funds for new centres which would bring together researchers with those who could apply the findings, either commercial operators or government agencies that could use the work for the public benefit. The first rounds of centres were a good mix of those with a profit orientation in such areas as building materials, and those aimed at a broader public benefit such as tropical pest management. The Howard government retained the Cooperative Research Centres program but restricted funding to centres with a narrow commercial focus. The Rudd and Gillard years returned to a broader emphasis, with funding of centres in such areas as low-carbon futures. The Abbott government scrapped the program completely as part of its cutting funds for science generally, although several of the centres will continue for their contracted life. Transferring the very good Australian science into the growth industries of the twenty-first century will be crucial to our economic future. Abolishing a successful program that has been achieving useful transfers of knowledge was a remarkably short-sighted move.

The fundamental change since 1964 is that science was then seen as a public good. Governments funded CSIRO and other government laboratories, confident that their investment would flow through to community benefits. While university funds were tighter, there was also an acceptance that the community should fund basic research in the expectation that the knowledge would benefit us all. Now CSIRO and universities are increasingly expected to obtain research funds from sources other than the government, inevitably pushing researchers away from fundamental projects toward what is essentially consulting, applying their existing knowledge to specific problems.

THE WORKFORCE

The significant decline in manufacturing since *The Lucky Country* was published in 1964 has led to a steady loss of jobs in that sector. Less often remarked upon, but probably more significant in social terms, has been the equally dramatic loss of jobs in agriculture as a result of mechanisation. Where farmers were often milking their cows or harvesting their crops by hand, and using horses to plough their land, those tasks are now largely mechanised and thus require fewer workers. Small farms have gradually been swallowed up by larger ones to achieve economies of scale, reducing still further the size of the workforce. More importantly, the services in rural towns have been wound back as there are fewer farm workers buying groceries, educating their children, having their health problems resolved or buying stamps. Australia is now overwhelmingly a service economy. The traditionally productive sectors of mining, manufacturing, agriculture, forestry and fishing together now account for less than 20 per cent of the workforce. Much has been made of the so-called mining boom, which has employed significant numbers of people, but more people work in cafes, restaurants and takeaway food outlets than in the entire mining industry. With about 2 per cent of the workforce, mining has about the same number of employees as the real estate sector!

The nature of employment in the mining industry has caused serious social problems and some local economic issues. Traditionally, when a mine opened the operator would build houses and try to attract workers to live there. In remote locations, they would also construct facilities to improve the chances of recruiting workers. Broken Hill, Kalgoorlie and Mount Isa are long established examples of towns built around a mine, while Roxby Downs in South Australia is a more recent case. In the 1990s, some operators recognised that the size of their workforce would not allow them to have the critical mass needed for good facilities, especially schools for workers' children, so they moved to a fly-in-fly-out model, or FIFO as it has become known. They argued this would allow the workers to establish their family homes in large towns or cities which had the range of facilities their families needed. Many of the mining operations in Queensland and Western Australia now work on this model. Thousands of workers catch early morning flights from Perth, Townsville or Brisbane to do their one-week or ten-day shift at the mine. It is a financially attractive model for the mine owners, but there have been several recent studies pointing to serious social problems for the workforce, leading to high levels of substance abuse, family break-ups, mental health problems and suicides. The other economic problem caused by the increasing importance of mining in some regions is that modern mines are highly capital-intensive, so labour costs are relatively small. That means mine owners are prepared to pay high wages to attract workers to the difficult conditions. In turn, that means that mine workers can afford to pay much more for accommodation than such public sector workers as police officers, teachers, nurses and paramedics. This has caused the serious problem in mining areas that essential service workers find it almost impossible to get housing they can afford.

Within our cities, more and more of the workforce is engaged in the service industries. That in turn means that the jobs are scattered much more uniformly around the city rather than being concentrated in the CBD as they were in 1964. Some industries such as health care provide reasonable incomes and career prospects, but others like the hospitality industry usually do not. So an increasing fraction of the workforce has relatively insecure income and working conditions. Overall, the workforce is much more mobile than when Donald Horne wrote his book. At that time, it was quite common for people to join a company when they left school and work for that organisation until they retired at 65 and were ceremonially given a gold watch by their grateful employer to recognise their long and devoted service. That pattern is now very rare, with most people not just having many changes of employer, but also many changes in the work they are doing.

Technology has made obsolete many jobs which employed large numbers of people in 1964. Other jobs have not disappeared, but have required new skills. Plumbers now use plastic pipes rather than copper, and are likely to be required to install solar hot water systems rather than electric or gas devices. Personal assistants no longer take notes in shorthand or use typewriters, but are expected to be able to use sophisticated communications tecYology. Change is continually creating new work opportunities, but those jobs are increasingly likely to demand advanced skills, so a growing problem is the fraction of the workforce who are older and less well-educated. Many of the jobs that existed in 1964 for fit, strong young men with little education no longer exist, having been replaced by equipment. The miner or farmer of today is more likely to be using a keyboard than physical strength. So a poor education is now a permanent liability. These changes in the workforce, and the growing social dislocation they encourage, will only be magnified as Australia continues to become further enmeshed in the global economy.

THE 'FREE TRADE' DELUSION

The global financial crisis (GFC) of 2008 was widely seen as marking a full stop to the era of unlimited trust in market forces. US regulators had given free rein to the so-called sub-prime mortgage sector, lending generously to people with low incomes and little capacity to repay the loans. Increasing numbers of defaults led to the collapse of these lending schemes and the consequent unravelling of a whole series of interlinked financial arrangements around the world. Major banks and even small countries such as Iceland were caught up in the crisis, having been persuaded to invest in opportunities that turned out to be literally too good to be true. The reassessment was profound. I attended a Summit on the Global Agenda convened in Dubai later that year by the World Economic Forum (WEF). The WEF is no radical body. It is the big end of town at a global level, best known for its annual winter meetings in the Swiss town of Davos that attract business leaders and finance ministers from around the world. The 2008 summit also brought together economists and business figures, but the mix was leavened by some academics and scientists. While the discourse mainly centred on economic issues, there was a profound analysis of the underlying problems of assuming unlimited growth could continue in a finite system. The final statement from the summit noted that the recent crises of finance, fuel and food were 'the three canaries in the mine, the early warnings that the current economic system is not sustainable'. This should have been a wake-up call to governments around the world, a warning that the naïve trust in markets could lead only to serious problems. Australia's leaders appeared not to notice, while the commercial media continued to call for 'further reform', which was code for even more deregulation rather than a tightening of the over-generous provisions which had caused the global crisis.

Australia was less affected than most affluent countries by the global events, largely because the Rudd government responded with a massive boost in public spending. The government launched huge programs of public works to construct school buildings and install home loft insulation. These programs were rolled out hastily to counteract the economic fall-out from the crisis in the financial sector. In hindsight, the government's haste to keep the economy moving led them to overlook the precautions that should have been taken to ensure the quality of the work. There was subsequent media criticism of some private sector contractors for doing work that was over-priced or sloppy. A more serious issue was that some of these corporate cowboys endangered poorly trained workers; four young workmen died in electrical accidents as they installed the insulation. As well as public works, the government took the radical and unprecedented step of sending each taxpayer a cheque for $900 to encourage us to spend and keep the economy ticking over.

This achieved its objective of preventing the sort of recession which occurred in northern hemisphere economies, but it allowed opportunistic claims from the Coalition that the government had increased Australia's public debt.

Despite the warnings from the WEF, Australia's leaders continued to place great faith in what were dishonestly called 'free trade agreements'. Most did not amount to free trade at all, though they all waived some specific obstacles or lowered some tariff barriers. The implicit belief driving the negotiation of these agreements was that the Australian economy, and consequently our society, would benefit from further liberalising trade. Given that the previous changes had created losers as well as winners, any credible analysis would have recognised that further changes would do the same. In their acerbic book *How to Kill a Country: Australia's Devastating Trade Deal with the United States*, Linda Weiss, Elizabeth Thurbon and JoŸ Mathews exposed the negative impacts on Australia of the so-called Free Trade Agreement (FTA) with the USA which was negotiated in 2004. It is worth quoting a paragraph from their introduction:

> The days of being the 'lucky country' – even with the phrase's ironic overtones – are over. The FTA changes everything: our economic and social policy options, our international economic and political constraints and, ultimately, our sense of place that helps define who we are ... this FTA will turn us into an appendage of the United States ... a kind of Pacific Puerto Rico. This is not the future that we would have hoped for. And it is not the future that we had to have. There was a time in the 1990s when it looked as if Australia might have a different – and certainly more independent – future, carving out a series of strategic goals for itself. Instead, we have chosen a military and

economic alliance with the United States so all-embracing that our government cannot distinguish pro-Australian sentiment from anti-American. In signing away the capacity to shape our economic prospects we have also destroyed our capacity to act internationally as an independent player.

The book goes on to identify the specific problems for Australia's future that arose directly from the agreement. Medicines became more expensive and competition from generic pharmaceuticals was undermined. Royalty flows to the USA increased through increased government protection for US patents and copyrights. Our agricultural systems have become threatened by allowing overseas produce to have greater access to local markets, risking the introduction of new diseases and pests, while Australia's major produce exports will not see tariffs and quotas removed for many years. Australian governments will be forced to give US goods and services preference over local equivalents when procuring their needs. It is hard to imagine how even a besotted supporter of market fundamentalism could see this as a plus for Australia.

As it was being considered, the proposed agreement was referred to the Commonwealth parliament's Joint Standing Committee on Treaties. As is usual, the government of the day had a majority on that committee and their report said that they had 'determined that ratification is in Australia's national interest'. There was, of course, no detailed explanation of the assessment of cost and benefits that led the Coalition parties to conclude that the overall balance would be in our favour. A dissenting report from six other parliamentarians noted that the proposed treaty depended critically on 'the legislative, regulatory and administrative measures' that would be needed to implement it. The uncertainty about those measures led the minority to conclude cautiously that it was not possible at that point to determine whether it would be in the national interest to sign the proposed agreement. They expressed specific concerns about some obvious negatives: the possible environmental impacts of the treaty, the effect on the Pharmaceutical Benefits Scheme in general and the capacity to use generic medications in particular, the legislative safeguards for local content in Australian media and the capacity of local institutions to access copyright materials. A decade later, critics would say that the dissenters were right to worry about these issues and the Coalition politicians were mistaken in their conclusion that ratifying the treaty would be in Australia's national interest.

In 2015, the damage done by the decade-old FTA was compounded by secret negotiations for a new agreement to liberalise further trade in services. It is scandalous that even the Australian parliament was not in the loop. The negotiations were being conducted behind closed doors by officials of the Department of Foreign Affairs and Trade (DFAT), who gave evasive answers to pointed questions from members of parliamentary committees about the possible agreement. It was only through WikiLeaks obtaining and releasing draft text that the issue received any sort of public exposure. Basically, the government was colluding with the US administration to promote a Trade in Services Agreement which could include as many as 52 countries. As well as Australia and the USA, the draft treaty extends to Canada, South Korea, Japan, Taiwan and the whole European Union. It has been touted as 'the largest trade deal in history', since it would cover countries that together generate about two-thirds of global wealth. When forced to defend the proposal, trade minister Andrew Robb argued that it would 'open up new opportunities' for the financial services sector. In principle, the scheme set out in the leaked draft text would allow Australian companies freer access to the markets of Europe, Japan, Taiwan, South Korea and the USA. That clearly amounts to new opportunities for local entrepreneurs. But there are also costs. The treaty would allow Japanese, South Korean, Taiwanese, European and American companies in the broad services sector freer access to Australian markets. The text of the draft agreement suggests the government is happy to trade away long-established policies such as the 'four pillars' approach to banking. This policy has ensured that there are no takeovers to further reduce competition in the banking sector, dominated as it is by the Commonwealth Bank, ANZ, Westpac and NAB. Previous governments have allowed the entry of foreign competitors like HSBC and Citibank, but the draft agreement would go further down the path of allowing the overseas corporations potentially to take over the remaining large local banks. This is a very worrying step backwards. Analysts of completely different persuasions agree that the strong regulation of local banks was a significant factor that helped Australia to avoid the GFC. We certainly should not be weakening the system to accommodate foreign financial interests.

The Saturday Paper quoted Matthew Rimmer, a professor of intellectual property and innovation law at Queensland University of Tecÿology, as expressing concern about the 'huge potential footprint' of the draft agreement. He pointed out that even the Productivity Commission (PC) had criticised DFAT's failure to 'engage in a rigorous, open and transparent scrutiny of trade deals' like the proposed Trade in Services Agreement. It is an obvious worry because about 80 per cent of Australian jobs are now in the services sector. In any of the fields of health care, retail, education, legal and financial services, local companies could be forced to compete with overseas-owned enterprises that can afford to subsidise their local operations to put Australian providers out of business. It also opens the door still wider to tax avoidance practices such as transfer pricing. It became apparent in 2015 that large corporations like Microsoft and Apple were using creative schemes to avoid paying tax in Australia, such as having the local subsidiary buy their products at inflated prices from another arm of the company to reduce the apparent local profit. A broad-based agreement to liberalise trade in services would actively encourage such activities, to the detriment of both local companies and our government's tax revenue. If the corporations operating in Australia are able to avoid their tax responsibilities, citizens either have to pay higher taxes or accept a lower standard of publicly provided essential services.

The criticism by the PC is particularly significant, given that it is generally seen as dominated by economists who believe devoutly in neo-classical economics in general and trade liberalisation in particular. The 2015 White Paper on Agricultural Competitiveness quoted the PC as pointing out that 'Bilateral trade agreements might improve market access for some agricultural producers, but others inevitably miss out. Agreements almost always involve complex rules of origin offsetting access benefits and risk costly trade diversion.' Worse, from the viewpoint of those who favour trade liberalisation, *Crikey* cited a PC explanatory note stating that such bilateral agreements can actually slow down broader trade reform. A bilateral treaty encourages countries to keep some of their trade barriers to use as bargaining chips in future bilateral deals. In the 2014–15 Mid-Year Financial Outlook, the Australian government hailed its 'free trade agreements' with Korea, Japan and China as 'world-class, comprehensive agreements that substantially liberalise our trade with major markets, delivering significant benefits to Australian exporters, farmers, manufacturers and consumers'. This is really a statement of ideology rather than a hard-nosed assessment of the costs and benefits of the agreements. While the government lauds the 'enormous opportunities for Australian business to expand in the region', it overlooks the equal opportunity for Asian businesses to expand into Australia. One argument was that agreements with China, Japan and South Korea would go some way to levelling the playing field that had been grossly tilted by JoŸ Howard's deal with the USA. But impartial analysts cautioned against overblown hopes about the benefits of such trade agreements, noting that the Treasury forecast the total combined effect of the three proposed deals with giant Asian economies could possibly add 0.05 per cent to the Australian economy by 2035. Given that such estimates have usually overstated the benefits of trade agreements and ignored the costs, we should regard Treasury's forecast as being at the optimistic end of the credible range of estimates. The agreements certainly won't measurably improve our standard of living.

There are also costs associated with such a trade agreement. Trade unions campaigned against some of the provisions of the proposed bilateral arrangement with China. One specific provision that concerned them was the concession for a Chinese company that invested $150 million or more in a project to bring in 'temporary workers' for that scheme. There would apparently be no requirement to attempt to recruit local workers or to meet Australian standards of workforce health and safety. As in other agreements being considered behind closed Canberra doors, there did not appear to be a time limit on the nature of 'temporary' work. It could, for example, be argued that a new mine had a limited life of 30 years, so the mining jobs would all be temporary. The draft agreement would also give Chinese companies the right to sue Australian governments, state, territory or Commonwealth, if they passed laws that the companies believed had a negative effect on them. That means, for example, that a new law to tighten up environmental protection or to require those companies to meet other local standards could allow the Chinese company to obtain financial compensation for their increased costs. Australian taxpayers will foot the bill if our future governments require the overseas company to meet the standards we expect of local enterprises.

In 2015, the Australian government was enthusiastically participating in an extremely ambitious US-led proposition called the Trans-Pacific Partnership (TPP). The other countries involved were Brunei, Chile, Canada, Japan, Malaysia, Mexico, New Zealand, Peru, Singapore and Vietnam. Opponents of the proposed deal were pointing out that it would, like the proposed bilateral agreement with China, allow international corporations to take legal action if they were disadvantaged by local policies. Such lawsuits are proceeding in other jurisdictions as a result of trade agreements. The largest under way in 2015 was action by the nuclear industry, trying either to reverse the German decision to phase out nuclear power or obtain billions of euros in compensation for the loss of anticipated business. In similar terms, when Quebec banned hydraulic fracturing of rock seams for gas extraction, a foreign company filed a $250 million claim for compensation in a Canadian court. It has been reported that it is costing the Australian government many millions of dollars to defend our plain packaging laws against legal action brought by a large tobacco company, using the dispute provisions of the earlier trade agreement with Hong Kong. These examples support the argument that such deals undermine our capacity to make our own laws in our own interests. In fact, it seems clear from the information leaked about the secret negotiations that the proposed treaty would quite explicitly give overseas-based corporations a privileged position in the Australian legal system.

Again, it is almost impossible to make a case that such a deal would advance our national interest. In fact, it will be a major step backwards if we are unable to make our own decisions about environmental standards, workplace safety and consumer protection. Even *The Australian*, which characteristically hailed the TPP on its front page as the producer of a new age of prosperity, had much more cautious analysis in its financial pages. The obvious point is that the fine print of the agreement, which was not made public when the deal was announced, would determine whether the benefits to Australia will exceed the costs. Even when the fine print is made public, there will still be uncertainty about how the agreement will be used by Australian and overseas corporations.

OUR CRITICAL DEPENDENCE ON THE GLOBALISED ECONOMY

The level of integration of the global economy presents a new problem, as the GFC exemplified. Because financial institutions around the world had been seduced by promises of huge potential profits from US sub-prime mortgages, when that market collapsed it had knock-on effects all around the world, as discussed earlier. Long-established financial institutions like the Bank of Scotland had to be rescued by the UK government, while the public finances of the entire country of Iceland were threatened by the rash investments of their Treasury. In similar terms, in 2015 there was frantic speculation about the possible impacts on Australia of a downturn in the Chinese stock market. In a rational world, gains and losses by the speculators in what is almost a Chinese casino should have little impact on Australia. But the Australian economy is now so critically dependent on Chinese purchases of our raw materials that our large companies suddenly look less profitable if China cuts back. Similarly, currency speculators apparently sold Australian dollars after the July 2015 Greek referendum to buy what were seen as stronger currencies like the Japanese yen and the US dollar. The consequent reduction in the value of the Australian dollar affected our exports, increasing the return to the companies selling our minerals overseas at prices set in US dollars. It also had an impact on our imports, increasing the prices to Australian consumers of manufactured goods from overseas. Australia is no longer an island in economic terms. Our capacity to make our own decisions about our economic direction and our social institutions has been seriously compromised by the enthusiasm of successive governments to integrate Australia into the global economic system. ALP politicians are just as keen as Coalition figures to encourage foreign investment, seeming to worry only when the overseas interests are state-owned organisations like some of those from China rather than private corporations from the USA or Europe. Even our productive land is being sold to overseas interests. In 2015, a Chinese billionaire, Xingfa Ma, added two large cattle properties on the Queensland–Northern Territory border to his portfolio which already included Balfour Downs, Emu Downs and Wandanya Station in Western Australia.

Iron ore and coal exports

As Australia still has the economic structure of a Third World country, exporting raw materials to pay for the imports we aren't clever enough to make for ourselves, we are critically dependent on the appetite of world markets for our resources. Two huge problems have emerged as a direct consequence. The first is that the world price for iron ore, our largest single export, has roughly halved in value over the last few years. As always, there is not one simple cause. One factor is that the Chinese economy has slowed, or at least its growth has become less rapid than it had been for several years, which has significantly reduced world demand for iron ore. Another factor is that the previous high prices had both attracted new producers into the industry and emboldened the largest producers, Rio Tinto and BHP Billiton, to expand production. With supply increasing and demand slowing, there has been an inevitable imbalance which has led to the price falling. That is a problem for the iron-ore exporters, but it is also a problem for state and Commonwealth governments who rely on revenue from the industry.

The second huge problem is the export coal industry. For decades, state and Commonwealth governments have devoted great efforts to encouraging the industry to expand. Now climate change has put the whole future of that industry in doubt. China, one of our larger customers, has already cut back significantly on coal burning. Electricity use increased in the first half of 2015, but coal use dropped 5 per cent. The projected reduction in China's coal use over the two-year period 2014–15 is about 250 million tonnes, roughly equivalent to Australia's total exports. Other countries are seriously questioning planned new investments. In 2014, a new movement took off encouraging investors to divest their interests in the coal industry. It was partly driven by the growing movement for ethical investment, adding fossil fuels to their longstanding avoidance of tobacco, weapons and uranium. That driving force was supplemented by hard-nosed financial analysts who saw demand for coal dropping, leading them to conclude that there would be little chance of good financial returns. When the Australian National University decided to withdraw its investments in the coal industry, there was an almost hysterical reaction from the government and the resources industry, obviously recognising that the example could well be followed by other investors.

It was revealed by the incoming ALP government in Queensland that the state Treasury had warned the Newman government against supporting the proposed giant Carmichael mine in the Galilee Basin, on the basis that the project was a very dubious proposition in strict financial terms, but the government was so committed to the coal industry that it went ahead with guarantees of support from public funds. The project is still in doubt, with a series of financial institutions declining to provide funds, but the Queensland and Commonwealth governments have promised to expand the Abbot Point coal-loading facility to improve the prospects of the mine becoming viable. A new large mine requires a production life of 30 or 40 years to recoup the initial capital investment and return a profit. It would be a very brave investor who would be sure of a new coal mine operating to at least 2050 to return their capital. Advocates for the resources industry were bravely talking about Australian coal being superior to coal from other countries and therefore especially attractive, but the argument is very unconvincing. Certainly some leading global finance experts such as Satyajit Das are now warning against investment in new large coal mines, strictly on the grounds of risk that the projects will not be able to repay their capital costs.

As with iron ore, state and Commonwealth governments now rely heavily on revenue from coal exports, so they are prepared to hold the climate change telescope to their collective blind eye and still see a bright future for the coal industry. Even former executives in that sector are now sounding a warning against that naïve optimism. Ian Dunlop, a former coal company executive and industry leader, ran an unsuccessful campaign for election to the board of BHP Billiton in 2014, arguing that the existing board was neglecting its fiduciary duty by assuming continued expansion of coal exports. He argued that the board members may be exposing themselves to the risk of legal action when they prove to have wasted corporate money on new export coal mines. This issue will not go away.

Globally, renewables accounted for more than half of all the new electricity capacity installed in 2014. In 2015, the Chinese government announced its 2020 energy targets. They include 350 gigawatts (GW) of hydro-electricity, 200 GW of wind power, 100 GW of solar and 58 GW of nuclear power. (For comparison, Australia's total installed electricity capacity is about 50 GW.) Those figures show that China, as one observer said, 'can only be described as an emerging renewables superpower', with wind and solar energy rapidly exceeding nuclear. Coal is being phased out; as noted earlier, China's coal use in 2016 will be 250 million tonnes less than the 2014 figure. Only those in deep denial could be placing their hopes for a bright economic future on further expansion of coal exports; the most likely future is a steady decline from present levels as the world phases out coal-fired electricity. The reducing sales volume is likely to be compounded by falling prices as supply exceeds demand, leading to very bleak financial outcomes for the coal industry. In 2015, the Australian Coal Association reported that the majority of mines producing steaming coal were operating at a loss and the share value of coal exporters was down to about 30 per cent of the 2010 figure.

Uranium exports

The uranium industry has a similar problem. The Australian export industry expanded in the late decades of the twentieth century, until Chernobyl spread radioactive pollution across a wide area of Europe in 1986 and orders for new nuclear power stations were cancelled or deferred in response to public concern about safety. The industry looked to be in terminal decline.

Then a group in the UK had the bright idea of re-badging nuclear power as a low-carbon source of electricity. This meant the nuclear industry had to embrace the cause of environmental critics it had been fighting for decades, but desperate times call for desperate measures. Some well-credentialled Australian engineers, backed by the Murdoch press, were saying that they were not convinced that human activity was changing the global climate and the evidence certainly didn't justify slowing down coal exports. At the same time, they began saying that the problem was so critical we should panic and build nuclear power stations to reduce the release of greenhouse gases from electricity generation! The argument, dubious as it was, gained some traction in western Europe and was given some support in Australia by the Howard government, as discussed earlier.

Then the Fukushima accident happened. Even if the reactors concerned had not been partially fuelled by Australian uranium, that incident would still have been a serious blow to the industry. Not only did it cause some countries who were thinking of possibly building nuclear power stations to revise those plans, it also caused other countries to close existing power stations or start planning to phase them out. The entire Japanese nuclear power industry was suspended until mid-2015, four years after Fukushima. Japan has more than 40 other nuclear reactors, but public hostility is still deterring successive governments from bringing those power stations back on line. In late 2015, only two had been recommissioned. Germany has decided to phase out its nuclear power stations, requiring a massive investment in solar and wind; that northern European country now has more installed solar power than Australia. The end result of these political responses to the Fukushima accident is that the global demand for uranium has stalled, leading to a drop in the market price. Users have become reluctant to sign long-term contracts, believing the price may fall further. The long-planned expansion of the Olympic Dam mine in South Australia has been postponed, with no real sign of it being restarted. Rio Tinto has cancelled its proposal to extend the life of the Ranger uranium mine by developing an underground operation. Other planned uranium mines in Western Australia have also been mothballed. So the industry faces both a reduced volume of sales and lower prices, together making its economic return questionable. As with coal and iron ore, governments relying on projected royalty income from the mining projects are looking glumly at the red ink on their forward estimates. It is just another example of the problem of the short-sighted approach to economic development, relying on commodity exports which have their prices set by world markets we cannot control.

The collapse of the BHP Billiton proposal to expand the Olympic Dam operation was seen by the SA government as a serious blow to its economic future. The state had seen support for the local car industry withdrawn by the Abbott government, leading all the state's manufacturers, one by one, to announce the end of local production. The promised building of the next generation of submarines in the state was also in doubt after the Abbott government's first defence minister, David JoŸston, said in 2014 that he would not trust an Adelaide-based submarine-building company to build a canoe! So South Australia appeared desperate to find a new industry to provide large numbers of jobs. Successive governments had placed their faith in BHP Billiton's proposal to expand the Olympic Dam mine by an operation of almost unimaginable size. The expansion would have required shifting something like five cubic kilometres of rock to reach the ore body and would have created the largest hole on the planet, about four kilometres across and an amazing kilometre deep. The SA government was publicly championing the benefits of the project, even before it had conducted a perfunctory environmental impact assessment. The fact that the project would have created the world's largest pile of low-level radioactive waste in its mine tailings was seen as irrelevant by a government eager to have a large project on the horizon. Most observers saw this desperation for a new industry as the prime motivation for establishing a royal commission into the nuclear industry, discussed in an earlier chapter, as pro-nuclear activists had been claiming for some time that there are huge economic opportunities in the field of radioactive waste management. It is an interesting argument. When the Howard government tried to establish a repository for low-level radioactive waste in a remote area of the state, the SA government of the day tapped into public concern and successfully opposed the proposal. At the time, critics said that it was irrational to be happy to have a huge uranium mine in the state, generating radioactive tailings that will need to be managed for centuries, while being opposed to an engineered site for low-level waste from Lucas Heights, near Sydney, and other sites around the country.

The contradiction links back to the earlier discussion of the 1976 report into the Ranger mine. That report said that the two problems with exporting uranium were the production of radioactive waste and the risk of fissile material being turned into weapons. At a 1977 public forum discussing the report, the possibility was raised that Australia could take an integrated approach to avoid these problems. Rather than selling uranium, one scientist suggested, we could process the mineral into reactor fuel elements to be leased to potential users, on the condition that they would be returned after use for disposal. This approach would ensure both that the waste was managed responsibly and that fissile material was not diverted for weapons production. The mining company executives on the panel at that forum almost dived under the table, so appalled were they by the idea. I interpreted the executives' hostility as reflecting their interpretation of the public mood and the precarious social licence for the industry. People are prepared to allow uranium mining and exporting, as it creates local jobs and pays modest royalties to governments. However, this acceptance does not extend to taking responsibility for its end products of radioactive waste and the potential to build nuclear weapons. So the mining companies were not at all interested at that time in the idea of the spent fuel rods being returned to Australia.

That view has not changed. I am grateful to SA environmental activist David Noonan for drawing my attention to some interesting paragraphs in BHP Billiton's submission to the Uranium Mining, Processing and Nuclear Energy Review commissioned by JoŸ Howard in 2006:

> We do not believe that conversion and enrichment would be commercially viable in Australia ... Nor do we believe any government imposed requirement to lease fuel, as distinct from acquiring uranium would be acceptable to its major customers ... BHP Billiton believes that there is neither a commercial nor a non-proliferation case for it to become involved in front-end processing or for mandating the development of fuel leasing services in Australia ...
>
> There is no evidence that a change to current Australian Government policies to facilitate domestic enrichment, fuel leasing and high level waste disposal would lead to significant economic opportunities or reduce proliferation risks in the foreseeable future ... It would also put at risk our reputation with customers of being a reliable supplier of uranium concentrates and our ability to enter into the long term supply arrangements that underpin expansion of uranium mining. Noting that a

nuclear fuel leasing industry, 'if permitted by the regulatory framework', is most unlikely to be commercially viable, BHP Billiton would strongly oppose any policies to artificially support the premature development of such an industry by requiring BHP Billiton's customers to use Australian conversion, enrichment or fabrication services ... It would put customer relations and the investments those underpin at risk.

This discussion is significant because only a very small number of pro-nuclear enthusiasts see a role for nuclear power in any part of this country. It is very hard to twist the data for such a project to make economic sense and, after Fukushima, it seems unlikely any community would be enthusiastic to host a nuclear power station. So most observers in South Australia see the real political agenda of the royal commission as softening up the public to accept radioactive waste being taken to the state, first from other parts of Australia. Some also see northern hemisphere countries still facing intractable community opposition to proposals to store their local waste and argue that they may be desperate enough to pay large sums to Australia to solve their problem by setting up a global waste facility. As I mentioned earlier, one local senator was even arguing that this could prove such an economic bonanza that the local community would enjoy free electricity: an argument that I had not heard since the heady days of nuclear boosterism 60 years ago!

Australia's economic development prospects have been implicitly based on the assumption that we will earn increasing export income from iron ore, coal, uranium and other metals to pay for the manufactured goods we do not make for ourselves. That is now looking a very dubious strategy. The difficulty of relying on commodity exports is magnified by the global changes that appear increasingly likely.

ECONOMY

TACKLING THE LOOMING GLOBAL CRISIS

The 2008 Summit on the Global Agenda concluded that the world was facing a perfect storm with the convergence of several critical issues. The financial crisis of that year, discussed earlier, came on top of other complex and urgent linked problems: climate change, water security, food security and energy security. The WEF convened the summit in association with the Dubai government. The meeting was planned long before the GFC and the invitation list was not therefore specifically tailored to focus on that event, but the crisis did sharpen the minds of the economists and politicians. The panels dealing with economic and financial issues were all doom and gloom, saying that the outlook was worse than at any time in living memory. The conclusions from the groups dealing with social and environmental issues were not much brighter: biodiversity in crisis, no coherent plan to tackle climate change, poverty and disadvantage worsening. That led to the inevitable conclusion that business-as-usual is not an option. The situation demands new approaches, new tecÿologies and new institutional arrangements. The urgency of the situation demanded a response and the summit saw the crisis stimulating a review of practices that are now inappropriate. I worry that it took the GFC to make leaders aware of the need for change. Reports on the *Global Environmental Outlook* had been saying since the late 1990s that postponing action was not an option. The *Millennium Assessment* report underlined the message that a concerted approach is needed. Since those reports focused mainly on social and environmental problems, they got no serious attention from decision-makers, who are more concerned with economic issues. Only now, with the economic outlook as bleak as the social and environmental indicators have been for a decade or more, are some decision-makers getting the message that changes are needed, while some still remain oblivious to the problems.

Like Kevin Rudd's 2020 Summit, held shortly after he was elected in 2007, the 2008 Summit on the Global Agenda was impressive just for happening. It brought together a diverse group, although I would have liked it to be more diverse. The gender balance was poor. Africa, Asia and Latin America were conspicuously under-represented, leading one observer to suggest that the World Economic Forum is really the North Atlantic Economic Forum. The plenary sessions were dominated by the usual suspects, US men well past the first flush of youth. And the conclusions from most of the groups did not disturb the world view of the dinosaurs, many of whom were still urging us to close our minds and trust the market to deliver a better world. The 700 participants were divided into nearly 70 groups for detailed discussion. I was, appropriately enough, in the group on the future of Australia. While we could have discussed that topic without leaving home, we would not have been working in the broader context of the global gathering and our thoughts would not have been informing those of the other groups. We reinforced the message that current global institutions are inadequate for the challenges we now face. The best hope for the future, we said, lies in a process of social learning to develop a 'green economy'.

Our views were consistent with most of the contributions in the final plenary session. We were urged to 'let go of the old ways': coal, nuclear power, religions and seeing GDP growth as a measure of progress. We need to identify the critical limits of natural systems and ensure our development is within those limits. 'It's the climate, stupid!' said one contributor, reinforcing the repeated observation that the continuing challenge of climate change was much more important than the essentially temporary

GFC. Another speaker urged us to recognise that 'the crises are interconnected'. 'Fundamental change is long overdue', said yet another. We were urged to democratise decision-making, empowering the disadvantaged to allow 'bottom-up' responses rather than assuming the world can be controlled by existing elites. The need for a global approach demands that individual nations sacrifice some of their sovereignty for the common good. The panel dealing with global governance said explicitly that the existing institutions are inadequate for the challenges we now face as a global community, while the health groups warned that we are not prepared for future pandemics which they argued are made inevitable by mass transport.

As part of the process in Dubai, we each spent a couple of hours sharing ideas with other panels. I was particularly interested in the conclusions of the groups that considered climate change, alternative energy and 'ecosystems and biodiversity'. The climate change group stressed the urgency of a global approach to the problem. There was heartening talk of a possible summit meeting between Barack Obama and Chinese leaders to discuss climate change; unlike other issues like trade where there is conflict between the USA and China, they share an interest in finding a way forward that is acceptable to both parties. Subsequent developments have underlined the critical importance of the two global superpowers in building momentum toward a possible global response to climate change. Obama mentioned 'a planet in peril' as one of the four big issues facing him, while other leaders acknowledged that the GFC had not removed the need to slow down climate change. It was a timely reminder. While the Rudd government's 2020 Summit in Canberra endorsed a comprehensive approach to climate change and the Garnaut Climate Change Review study reminded the government of the urgency of the task, the resulting Green Paper was disappointingly limp. The Australian government seemed to have been spooked by the concerted campaign run by big polluters, suggesting the sky would fall if we didn't continue their generous treatment. While most people agree that our responses to climate change should not ignore the economic impacts of change, it would be naïve to assume that our present arrangements are so perfect they must be maintained at any cost. The special pleading of the aluminium industry is especially outrageous as it is mostly overseas-owned and making good profits on the back of huge subsidies from Australian taxpayers. A study by the Australian Conservation Foundation showed that the treatment proposed in the Green Paper would have amounted to paying hundreds of millions of our tax dollars to profitable overseas-owned companies like Rio Tinto. Since then the policy response has gone further backward in Australia, with the Coalition government's 'direct action' approach explicitly handing out public funds to the biggest polluters. Rather than making polluters pay, the scheme will actually give government money to companies that say they will reduce their pollution, with no effective enforcement mechanism to ensure that happens.

The alternative energy group in Dubai took an encouraging systemic view, recognising that the task is not to increase supply but to improve the delivery of energy-related services. So the most cost-effective alternative is not any form of supply, but improving the efficiency of turning the existing energy supply into lighting, heating, cooking, buildings and transport. Even the struggling US car industry seems to be finally getting the message that there is no future in building dinosaur vehicles, with GM and Ford losing billions and the survival of Chrysler in serious doubt. The Australian car industry finally succumbed to the increasing tendency of our local motorists to buy imported cars, especially more efficient Japanese and Korean models, rather than the less efficient Holdens and Fords.

The recommendations of the Dubai panel concerned with ecosystems and biodiversity reminded me that we are actually doing quite well in Australia. There needs to be a systems approach to our scientific assessment, moving beyond the traditional silos of disciplines to explore interactions and develop integrated solutions. We have already moved in that direction with our *State of the Environment* reporting. Second, the group said, there is a critical need for better metrics, indicators of the state of natural systems or our demands on them. There was at that time real interest in Canberra in the idea of developing a system of natural resource accounts, so we understand the state of those assets. Unfortunately, those sorts of progressive ideas were rejected by the Abbott government, content to engage in simplistic slogans about borders and debt. Ideas like the ecological footprint convey clearly the scale of our impact, demonstrating that we are using much more than the sustainable productivity of natural systems. The ecosystem panel's third recommendation was to develop a range of tools to change behaviour: reform of existing subsidies, appropriate pricing of assets like water or burdens like carbon dioxide releases, targets for renewable energy supply and certification of natural products to influence consumer demand. Again, this principle has been accepted in Australia where we have targets for renewable energy and had introduced a pricing scheme to discourage polluting industries. The biggest problem in this area is reform of subsidies, a change that demands political will because those who benefit will always resist being weaned from the public teat. One interesting proposal was to develop ways of paying for delivery of 'ecosystem services'. The argument is that we now pay farmers for their marketable products, food and fibre, but the land also provides habitat, water storage, oxygen from plant respiration, windbreaks and changes to rainfall patterns. If we want farmers to reduce production to supply these services, arguably they should be compensated for their financial sacrifice. Finally, governance must be improved. For all the limitations of the global agreement to slow climate change, it is seen as being much more effective than the Convention on Biological Diversity and a model for the approach needed: 'a new governance structure with stronger links to the long-term economic and financial implications of the loss of natural capital'. So that panel reinforced my feeling that the rest of the world has at least as much to learn from Australia as we do from them. Our group risked antagonising the northern hemisphere heavyweights, who certainly don't think they can learn from us, by pointing that out in our report.

While the 2008 Summit on the Global Agenda produced a mountain of good ideas, the real problem is implementation. We should be familiar with this issue because of the almost complete failure to implement the ideas of our own 2020 Summit. At least Kevin Rudd and his ministers were at the local summit and heard the discussion, although they were clearly primed to try to stop us rocking the boat. In the group I was part of, government minister Penny Wong seemed desperate to ensure that our recommendations were not critical of the coal industry. Her report to the final plenary session even noted the objection of a small group from the mining industry to the overwhelming majority view that we should never again build new coal-fired power stations. In the case of the WEF, it could only bring ideas to the attention of world leaders when they subsequently met at Davos the following January. Still, I left Dubai feeling the WEF understood the need to evolve beyond the recent obsession with markets and economic growth. That may be the enduring benefit of their summit: the recognition that the 'Washington consensus', with its narrow emphasis on market liberalisation, needed to be supplanted by what I called the 'Zurich consensus' – an integrated approach to environmental, social and economic development, as understood by various international bodies based in Switzerland. Other thinkers have argued that the post-2008 crisis will lead inexorably to a transformation of the global economy. In an article for *The Guardian* based on his 2015 book *Postcapitalism: A Guide to Our Future*, Paul Mason says:

> The 2008 crash wiped 13% off global production and 20% off global trade. Global growth became negative – on a scale where anything below +3% is counted as a recession. It produced, in the west, a depression phase longer than in 1929–33, and even now, amid a pallid recovery, has left mainstream economists terrified about the prospect of long-term stagnation. The aftershocks in Europe are tearing the continent apart.
>
> The solutions have been austerity plus monetary excess. But they are not working. In the worst-hit countries, the pension system has been destroyed, the retirement age is being hiked to 70, and education is being privatised so that graduates now face a lifetime of high debt. Services are being dismantled and infrastructure projects put on hold.
>
> Even now many people fail to grasp the true meaning of the word 'austerity'. Austerity is not eight years of spending cuts, as in the UK, or even the social catastrophe inflicted on Greece. It means driving the wages, social wages and living standards in the west down for decades until they meet those of the middle class in China and India on the way up.
>
> Meanwhile in the absence of any alternative model, the conditions for another crisis are being assembled. Real wages have fallen or remained stagnant in Japan, the southern

Eurozone, the US and UK. The shadow banking system has been reassembled, and is now bigger than it was in 2008. New rules demanding banks hold more reserves have been watered down or delayed. Meanwhile, flushed with free money, the 1% has got richer.

Neoliberalism, then, has morphed into a system programmed to inflict recurrent catastrophic failures.

The point about increasing inequality is a telling one. In 2015, Oxfam released data showing that the 85 richest individuals in the world, all of them billionaires, together have as much wealth as the poorest 3.5 billion of the human population! That sort of inequality is clearly not sustainable, so it is easy to see that it carries the risk of 'catastrophic failure'. But Mason makes a more fundamental point about the current economic transformation, which he argues is as radical as the change from feudalism to capitalism. He points out that the emerging economy is based on information, which is plentiful, whereas traditional economics has been based on factors of production which are intrinsically limited, such as land, labour and capital. He says, 'The main contradiction today is between the possibility of free, abundant goods and information, and a system of monopolies, banks and governments trying to keep things private, scarce and commercial. Everything comes down to the struggle between the network and the hierarchy: between old forms of society moulded around capitalism and new forms of society that prefigure what comes next.' At one level, this implies a utopian view of a new economic system. It also recognises that the old economic system, predicated on unlimited growth in a closed system, cannot be the basis of a viable future world. As Mason puts it, 'The democracy of riot squads, corrupt politicians, magnate-controlled newspapers and the surveillance state looks as phoney and fragile as East Germany did 30 years ago'. His vision 'is a project based on reason, evidence and testable designs, that cuts with the grain of history and is sustainable by the planet'.

A FUTURE WITHOUT ECONOMIC GROWTH?

The accumulating and accelerating problems have led thoughtful economists to question whether continued economic growth is desirable. At one level, this is not a new discussion. In 1980, the US economist Herman E Daly spoke at a Melbourne conference about his proposal for a steady-state economy. Daly has been a professor at various US universities and moved in the late 1980s to a senior role at the World Bank. His 1980 paper was published as a chapter in the book *Quarry Australia?* which is still on my shelves. He argued that the growth economy was a comparatively recent and inevitably temporary phenomenon, now putting the world on track for intractable problems. The only way of avoiding those issues, Daly argued, is to move purposefully over several years to an economy which is not predicated on continuing growth. He used the analogy of flight. A winged aircraft can stay in the air only if it is moving fast enough for the flow of air over the wings to generate lift. If its speed drops below the critical value, the aeroplane stalls and crashes. On the other hand, a helicopter is designed so that it can hover in one spot; it does not need forward motion to stay in the air. Daly said we can redesign the growth economy to be able to operate in a steady state, or we can watch it inexorably slow until it stalls and crashes.

A similar approach was taken by a Canadian professor called Peter Victor, whom I met when we both gave papers to the same conference in Italy a few years ago. He said that he had grown up believing the promises of economists that growth would eliminate poverty, reduce inequality and enable us to clean up the environment. He realised in his fifties that 30 years of rapid growth had not achieved any of those goals. In fact, poverty had not been eliminated, inequality had widened within and between countries, and our environmental problems had become steadily worse. He reminded me that one of the definitions of insanity is to keep doing what you have done before and expect a different result! So Victor embarked on an ambitious research project. He used an economic model similar to that used by the Canadian Treasury to analyse different possible futures for their economy. I was interested because his country has a similar economic structure to Australia, being dependent on commodity exports to pay for its imports of goods and services. Canada is also a country of similar size to Australia, it has about the same population and, as in Australia, that population is concentrated around the edges of the country where the climate is less severe. So we could apply the lessons of Canada to our situation.

Victor's work is summarised in his book *Managing without Growth: Slower by Design, Not Disaster.* He projected the current trajectory of economic growth and found critical problems would occur within a couple of decades: worsening environmental pollution, an accelerating contribution to climate change and serious social unrest caused by widening inequality. He then considered an alternative future in which growth was halted immediately, and found a different set of critical problems: unemployment reaching unacceptable levels, producing social unrest, and economic inability to solve environmental problems. So he explored futures in which the rate of growth is slowed over a few decades to give both a stable population and a steady-state economy. There would be less work in an economy that was not growing, so there would again be serious social unrest if there were not also policies to share the work more equally, such as reduced working hours. Environmental degradation would continue unless there were conscious policies to avoid it, such as a carbon price high enough to drive investment toward cleaner energy and encourage more efficient use: something like $200 a tonne of emitted carbon, about ten times the modest charge introduced by the Gillard government. With that integrated set of policies, Victor found, it would be possible to achieve a genuinely sustainable future with full employment, reduced inequality and environmental protection. We desperately need a similar study for Australia, exploring ways of slowing growth rather than persisting with the delusion that growth can continue forever. That approach is an important counter to the present situation in which decision-makers ignore both the short-term problems that are being directly caused by growth and the long-term problem that growth cannot continue forever in a finite system.

In 2014, the Academy of Science supported the Fenner Conference *Addicted to Growth?* on the specific issue of looking beyond growth to a stabilised future for Australia. Haydn Washington, a visiting fellow at the UNSW Institute of Environmental Studies, wrote a discussion paper for the conference, based on his forthcoming book *Demystifying Sustainability: Towards Real Solutions*. It concludes that continuing growth in population and resource use is simply not sustainable. It quotes Dennis Meadows, one of the co-authors of *The Limits to Growth*, and his co-workers as pointing out that the global economy is already far above a level that could be sustained: 'there is no credible, socially just, ecologically sustainable scenario of continually growing incomes for a world of 9 billion or more people'. That leads into a discussion of a possible future in which we have stabilised both our population and the level of resource use. This shows, as Washington puts it, 'there are good grounds for believing that there can be as many (perhaps more) jobs in a steady state economy as today'. This is a critical conclusion, as the most common objection to the idea of slowing economic growth is that there will be a catastrophic impact on our ability to provide jobs for those who want to work.

Washington points to the relatively successful example of Cuba, effectively a non-growth economy which has faced the huge problem of a trade embargo from the USA for nearly 60 years since the overthrow of the Batista government by Fidel Castro. Despite its problems and a much lower average income than we have, Cuba has an average life expectancy similar to ours, partly because of its being a much more equal society and partly because of a high level of public investment in health care which enables Cuba to send doctors and nurses to troubled areas around the world. Although Cuba still obviously has problems, including a lower standard of material wealth and poorer living conditions than we would see as acceptable, Washington argues that its example shows that humans 'can not only survive in a steady state economy, but still have high well-being'. He goes on to analyse the barriers to moving toward a steady-state economy, the most obvious being the vested interests that benefit from growth. These are substantial obstacles, especially in our political system which allows large donations to political parties and paid advertising to shift voter opinions. Most analysts were convinced that the spending of millions by the Palmer United Party was the main reason for its unprecedented rise from total obscurity to having four members elected in 2013. Similarly, the massive television campaign by the mining industry when the Rudd government proposed a tax on super-profits not only persuaded the government to back down, it also destabilised Rudd's leadership and played a role in his removal from the prime ministership. That campaign also gave the Australian public a totally misguided impression about the economic importance of the mining industry and the number of people it employs. Surveys find that the average Australian thinks that mining employs about 20 per cent of the workforce, rather than the 2 per cent it actually does. The public view of the sector's contribution to our economy is similarly inflated. That example illustrates the importance of tackling the existing barriers if we want to move toward a sustainable path of economic development.

Finally, Washington suggests a set of concrete steps to enable the creation of a new type of economy that is not predicated on endless growth. Critical elements include stabilising the population at a level that could be sustainably supported, moving over two decades to an economy based on renewable energy and efficient resource use, changing the tax system to reward efficiency and discourage wastefulness, removing the current subsidies for fossil fuel supply and use, restructuring the finance system, developing and using as a measure of economic success a Genuine Progress Indicator rather than persisting in the delusion that the Gross Domestic Product is a useful measure, and encouraging investment in sustainable activities. Such a future is entirely possible and represents a more constructive approach than hoping for endless growth. This would seem the best realignment of our current economic priorities if we are to have any hope of being a genuinely lucky country.

BALANCE

One can hope that events will liberate what is good and progressive in Australia, not perpetuate what is bad; that the relaxation and ease of life and the prosperity will grow; that the ideal of fraternalism will gradually extend to include Asian [people] ... Then, assuming huge advances in science that will make development possible where it now is not, Australia might really claim the name of continent, a continent in which ... more successfully than in the USA, a new nation will be created with values that have some relation to ordinary human aspiration.
—The Lucky Country, fifth edition, pp. 246–7

Donald Horne sounded three loud warnings in *The Lucky Country*: the need to accept the challenges of where Australia is on the map, the need for 'a bold redefinition of what the whole place adds up to now' and the need for a revolution in economic priorities 'especially by investing in education and science'. Fifty years later, there has been little or no progress toward those goals. Our place on the map is recognised only, as Horne observed, as providing an opportunity to sell our minerals and buy cheaply manufactured goods. There has certainly been no 'bold redefinition' of what Australia adds up to. While the demography of Australia has changed out of all recognition since Horne wrote his book, the changes have been a series of random accidents rather than the result of inclusive community discussion of our alternatives. Governments of both colours avoid public discussion on the social impacts of recent large-scale migration, recognising that it is a tricky issue which can easily be hijacked by those who want to encourage racist attitudes. Finally, there has been no revolution in economic priorities or investment in education and science; on the contrary, the old economic model of selling low-value commodities to pay for our imports has become more firmly entrenched, while successive governments have reduced funding for research and public education. We face a coming global crisis, a perfect storm of limited resources, serious environmental problems, widening inequality, economic instability and political tensions.

The future is very unlikely to be a smooth extension of the past. While a breakthrough to a desirable future is still possible, all the indicators suggest upheavals and disruption, a breakdown of civilised society rather than a smooth transition. We need to be prepared for global events we cannot control.

A GLOBAL VIEWPOINT

The head of the Roman Catholic Church, Pope Francis, released in 2015 his long-awaited encyclical *Laudato si'*. It reinforced the idea that a sustainable future has to include both social justice and a willingness to live within the limits of global systems. The pastoral letter was predictably dismissed by conservative elements, who made absurd claims that the Pope is a Marxist or uninformed about the science of environmental problems. Since those personal attacks are unlikely to be effective in the public debate, the Pope's arguments (and similar interventions by such public figures as Archbishop Desmond Tutu) will force those conservative voices to attempt to defend policies and approaches that appear indefensible. Robert Manne's reflection on the papal encyclical compared its potential impact with Al Gore's famous documentary *An Inconvenient Truth*. The intervention by Gore, a former US vice-president who was denied the presidency only by electoral malpractice in the state of Florida, had a very significant impact. He set out clearly the nature and scale of the problem of human impact on the climate system and then proposed as the solution a rapid shift to renewable energy technologies. As Manne observes, the papal letter also says that we face critical environmental problems: 'Doomsday predictions can no longer be met with irony or disdain. We may well be leaving to coming generations debris, desolation and filth. The pace of consumption, waste and environmental change has so stretched the planet's capacity that our contemporary lifestyle, unsustainable as it is, can only precipitate catastrophe.' It goes further and makes a more fundamental point that the shift to clean energy systems is a necessary condition for a sustainable future, but it will not be sufficient just to slow down climate change if we are serious about the broader goal of sustainability. That would address the environmental problem, leaving the social issues of inequality and injustice untouched. As Manne's review said: 'It is the poorer nations who are already paying and will continue to pay the main price as the climate crisis deepens ... To make progress in the interconnected struggle against global warming and global inequality, the encyclical also talks of the need for a world political authority.' Manne also noted the Pope's attack on the malaise of consumption: 'The greed and self-centredness which is instilled by the consumer culture of instant gratification is also incompatible with the idea of "limits" and thus with the idea of the existence of a "common good".'

Naomi Klein tackled the political issues of neoliberal economics and the power of corporations head-on in her book *This Changes Everything: Capitalism vs. the Climate*, in which she argued that cleaning up our energy supply system will only defer catastrophic changes if we don't get off the treadmill of growth. All of the gains from reducing energy use per head or pollution per unit of energy, she argued, will inevitably be swallowed up if we keep having more heads and increasing material consumption per head, but the entire global economic system is predicated on growth. Since the most powerful corporations in the world base their business model on a presumption of endless growth, Klein argued, moving toward a sustainable future unavoidably involves tackling the power of those corporations and their current ability to make and shape governments. In similar terms, the Pope made the obvious point that the distribution of wealth is at least as important as its generation. In so doing, he has challenged the existing economic order fundamentally. The whole approach of development economics has been to ignore the disparity between rich and poor nations, to concentrate on achieving economic growth and implicitly assure the disadvantaged that their needs will be met if growth is sufficiently rapid. But if the total sum of human consumption is already beyond what can be sustainably produced from natural systems, that approach cannot work, even in principle. The only way of providing a decent standard of living for the poor of the world within the limits of natural systems is for material consumption in the affluent countries to be scaled back.

This is possible in principle, though it is clearly a serious political challenge. As far back as 2000, the United Nations Children's Fund (UNICEF) calculated that the basic needs of everyone on Earth could be met by spending US$70–80 billion, which was about 10 per cent of the global military budget at that time. Since then, arms spending has continued to increase and is now measured in trillions of US dollars. In a 2012 review, *Opportunity Costs: Military Spending and the UN's Development Agenda*, Archer and Willi considered various attempts to estimate how much it would cost to ensure that every human had the basics for a secure and civilised life: clean water, adequate nutrition, sanitation, reasonable shelter, basic health care, education for children. It is hardly surprising that the studies they reviewed found the amounts of extra aid funding needed to achieve these goals would be enormous, ranging between about US$70 billion and almost US$200 billion. After all, several hundred million people don't have enough to eat, about a billion don't have reliable clean water, about 2 billion don't have sanitation, several hundred million have inadequate housing and so on. The study then compared the cost of providing for everyone's basic needs with the global military budget. While there is a degree of uncertainty about some of the figures, the crucial point is that only about 5 to 10 per cent of the obscene amounts spent on the military would be enough. Since the USA accounts for about half of the global military spending, it can be said with assurance that about 10 to 20 per cent of the US military budget alone would allow everyone on Earth to have their basic needs met. Just one visionary leader of the USA who decided to make the world less unequal could achieve that by trimming the country's military budget and using the money to provide for the basic needs of the world's most disadvantaged people. The Pope's point is that no amount of military force can perpetuate the massive injustices we now see. If people continue to see no future where they live, they will continue to pour across seas and national borders in search of a better life.

Robert Manne quotes the US author Bill McKibben as saying of the papal encyclical, 'My own sense, after spending the day reading this remarkable document, was of great relief ... This marks the first time that a person of great authority in our global culture has fully recognised the scale and depth of our crisis, and the consequent necessary rethinking of what it means to be fully human.' The critical question now is how the world responds to this challenge. As Manne notes, the papal letter said that we tend to use uncertainty, real or confected, as an excuse for inaction: 'As often occurs in periods of deep crisis which require bold decisions, we are tempted to think that what is happening is not entirely clear ... This is the way human beings contrive to feed their self-destructive vices: trying not to see them, trying not to acknowledge them, delaying the important decisions and pretending that nothing will happen.' Finally, and perhaps most importantly, Manne observes that *Laudato si'* includes a clear message of hope, which rests 'ultimately on a faith in certain enduring and unexpungeable qualities of what can only be called the human spirit'. The Pope suggested that an 'authentic humanity ... seems to dwell in the midst of the tecÿological culture, almost unnoticed, like a mist seeping gently beneath a closed door'. It is that 'authentic humanity' which provides the genuine grounds for a positive future, even if it is currently reduced to seeping under closed doors.

AUSTRALIA TOWARD 2050

In 2010, the Australian Academy of Science launched an ambitious project to start a conversation about our national future. The project was expertly guided by two outstanding interdisciplinary thinkers, CSIRO's Dr Michael Raupach and ANU's Professor Tony McMichael. Tragically, both of these great scientific leaders passed away before the project was completed, but it will stand as a permanent legacy of their vision and commitment to our country.

The first phase of the project brought 35 leading researchers together for a four-day workshop. The participants formed four interdisciplinary working groups. Two of these considered possible aspirations for Australia's future. Of these two, one considered the fundamental issues of systems resilience, to determine the parameters within which we need to work for a sustainable future. I was in the second group, which looked at social and cultural perspectives. The other two groups worked on what are essentially tools for helping to navigate our future, scenarios and quantitative models. The participants worked from a basic synthesis document prepared in advance by a steering committee and also had access to a set of background papers. Subsequently, the academy published summaries of the thinking of the four groups and an integrating chapter drawing together those ideas to develop projections of our shared future, along with the background papers. The report *Negotiating our Future: Living Scenarios for Australia to 2050*, is essential reading for anyone seriously thinking about Australia's future.

The project began from a basis you will understand from the previous chapters. It notes that 'exponential growth cannot go on forever in a finite system' and summarises the evidence that we are approaching limits: 'stresses are evident in many aspects of the planet's environment that are critical for life'. These observations lead to the inescapable conclusion that 'the world faces a new challenge in the 21st century: that of adapting the human enterprise, strongly shaped by centuries of near-continuous growth, to the realities of a finite planet'. The introductory paper then makes an equally important point, sufficiently important to quote the entire paragraph:

> The social challenges faced by societies around the world are as great as the environmental challenges. As the world has become more affluent, it has also become more unequal. Inequity in wellbeing, health and affluence has grown over the last two centuries: the richest are better off than ever before, while for the poorest, global development has been a curse rather than a blessing by many metrics. Socially equitable societies providing access to opportunity for all and fostering fairness and cooperation are sources of wellbeing, cultural enrichment, innovation and social stability in a heterogeneous, connected world. There is a great deal of empirical evidence that improving social equity helps societies to do better by numerous measures, including health, freedom from violence, wellbeing and social cohesion. Social equity is therefore just as important as environmental sustainability. In the 21st century, the finitude of the resources of Planet Earth will mean that neither can be fully achieved without the other.

As discussed in the previous chapter, the social and environmental trends are being 'profoundly affected by the dynamics of globalisation' so we need to take account of the interconnected world in exploring alternative futures for Australia. The global dynamics mean that, as the report observed, the future is 'uncertain, contested and ultimately shared'. It is uncertain because a wide range of futures are possible. Which one eventuates will be the result of decisions and actions taken by us and others around the world. It is contested because there are legitimate differences about pathways, even among those who agree on the desired outcome of an equitable and sustainable future. It is also obvious that not all those involved in decision-making at this time even agree on that basic concept. However, we will all ultimately share the future that is being created. How we farm in Australia affects the climate in China and how Chinese people farm affects the climate here. As both the 2008 GFC and the 2015 Greek crisis demonstrate, financial instability in one part of the world causes ripples around the globe. Social instability in Afghanistan or Iraq, or civil war in Syria, or drought and poverty in sub-Saharan Africa, cause desperate people to move by the hundreds of thousands in search of a better life. If it were true when John Donne wrote that nobody is an island, it is much more demonstrably true today.

We need to recognise the complexity of the problem. Arjun Appadurai had a useful insight in his 1990 essay 'Disjuncture and Difference in the Global Cultural Economy'. Rejecting existing models of the global cultural economy, he argued that it should be understood as 'a complex, overlapping order featuring fundamental disjunctures between economy, culture, and politics which we have barely begun to theorize'. The framework he proposed for exploring the disjunctures between economies, cultures and politics was premised on the relationships between five primary dimensions, which he labelled by analogy with landscapes: etÿoscapes, mediascapes, tecÿoscapes, financescapes and ideoscapes. These different dimensions of the global problem need to be separately analysed.

Assessing our assets

One approach to assessing our assets is what Jane Gleeson-White calls the six capitals. In her 2015 book *Six Capitals*, she argues that we need to move beyond the traditional accounting practice of measuring the funds available to an enterprise. She draws on the 2013 work of the International Integrated Reporting Council (IIRC), which suggested that enterprises that want to be sustainable need to move beyond traditional accounting practice to consider six types of capital:

- *Financial capital*: as traditionally recorded, the funds available to an organisation
- *Manufactured capital*: physical objects that enable the organisation to operate, such as buildings, equipment and infrastructure
- *Intellectual capital*: knowledge-based intangibles such as intellectual property, copyrights, patents and licences
- *Human capital*: 'the skills, abilities, experience, motivation, intelligence, health and productivity' of the organisation's people
- *Social capital*: institutions and relationships within and between communities, including the brand and reputation of the organisation as well as the extent to which it is trusted by others
- *Natural capital*: the environmental resources and processes that enable the organisation to operate and support its prosperity.

Gleeson-White argues that 'we have privileged financial capital above every other value on earth, including the value of nature and of human beings and our communities', leading to a situation in which we are literally straining the ecological systems which support us 'to fuel our fixation with economic growth'. She points to the IIRC as 'the first concerted effort on a global scale to systematically address this problem'. However, she recognises the logical inconsistency at the heart of this model. It leads inexorably to assessing the other five capitals in the language of finance. But we cannot trade off one against the other. As I argued earlier in this book, no amount of wealth will bring back an extinct species or restore the productivity of degraded land on any reasonable timescale. For the six capitals model to help us, corporations need to evolve from their fixation on finance and shareholder value to embrace the benefits of considering natural systems, human capital and social capital. That relationship is discussed further in the last section of this book. So Gleeson-White champions the emergence of 'benefit corporations', which have to report annually on their social and environmental performance as well as their financial record. Rather than being legally liable if it reduces its profit to act responsibly, as a traditional corporation can be, it will be held accountable for its overall performance. That means that the value of its operation can't be measured simply in dollars, or even in numerical indicators of environmental responsibility such as carbon dioxide emitted per dollar of revenue: 'the accountants of the future will be as much story tellers as bean counters'.

As well as the stocks of various forms of capital, the Academy of Science report emphasises the need to be aware of interactions and feedback between different elements. We have long been aware at a superficial level of the existence of vicious and virtuous cycles. A vicious cycle exists when one poor outcome increases the chance of another. The report itemises some obvious examples such as poverty, homelessness, unemployment, violence, poor education and health problems, saying that 'these factors reinforce each other in disadvantaged communities, leading to a spiral of suffering and loss of wellbeing that can propagate from generation to generation'. We can also identify examples of virtuous circles: 'declines in youth unemployment leading to reduced homelessness, violence and rates of imprisonment and, in turn, to improved wellbeing and opportunity for the children of that generation'. A second example is that progressive policies could lead to more efficient use of natural resources, resulting in both economic gains and improved security of access to resources, which would in turn relieve pressures on the natural world. The report makes the obvious plea to recognise these complexities and try to find pathways that are beneficial at all levels and reinforce desirable trends.

It spells out our starting position, in terms of the various capitals. As far as the environment goes, 'Australia is unsustainably mining its high endowment of natural capital', citing the high rate of species loss, the over-allocation of water resources in southern regions, our large contribution to climate change and the likelihood that most of our valuable mineral resources will be exhausted this century. We have a good base of manufactured capital, but the failure to keep pace with our rapidly growing population is eroding this asset. We have low levels of investment in knowledge capital and 'the national priority placed on advanced knowledge development is low'. In terms of human capital, most Australians enjoy good health and our life expectancy has continued to increase, but there are pockets of serious and entrenched disadvantage. As far as social capital goes, we have 'broadly effective governance mechanism and functional institutions' as well as 'low levels of homelessness and inter-personal violence, high literacy and numeracy and good school retention rates'. On the other hand, 'inequality is high by OECD standards and increasing'. This problem has contributed directly to outbreaks of xenophobia as demonstrated by the July 2015 Reclaim Australia rallies. We have also failed to come to grips with 'the chronic disadvantage suffered by Indigenous Australians'.

Resilience, social and cultural factors

The working group discussing resilience began by stressing its importance as Australia develops, since 'our response in the face of disturbances and change will be a key determinant of the wellbeing of the Australian population'. They went on to ask some critical questions. What aspects of Australia are resilient to what kinds of disturbances? Are there identifiable broad general characteristics that will improve our capacity to respond to a variety of potential shocks? How might we develop the capacity to adapt to and shape change? They explored these questions through specific case studies. The consequences of the severe 1997–2009 drought in south-eastern Australia were studied, showing that the agricultural sector was much better able to withstand that serious external pressure because of a range of factors that improved its resilience: a water trading regime, access to groundwater, altered farm management practices and off-farm income, including government assistance. The group concluded that 'the adaptive capacity that saw Australia through the drought was the product of previous investment in financial, human and social capital, at scales that ranged from the individual to the national'. Even though the drought imposed substantial costs, especially at the local level, 'the system as a whole … came through relatively unscathed' – but the group noted that the maintenance of food security and overall farm revenue came at considerable cost to social and ecological capital.

The second case study was the increase in obesity. Where less than 8 per cent of the population were classified as obese in 1980, by 2006 the figure was 23 per cent. As obesity is linked to a wide range of health problems, it comes at a serious economic cost, estimated at over $50 billion in 2008. The root cause is a relatively small imbalance between food energy consumed and energy expended in living. The imbalance is small enough that quite modest changes like walking an extra 15 minutes each day and eating slightly less would alter the picture. But a number of forces make those apparently modest changes difficult: 'the sedentary nature of work, leisure and travel, and the ready availability and low cost of energy-dense foods' are obvious contributors.

Since there is no single cause, making population health more resilient arguably requires a broad systems approach. As a specific example, urban people would be more active if planning led to more of the services they use every day being within easy access on foot. They would also get more exercise if there was good public transport for longer journeys, because using public transport rather than a car usually requires walking further to and from the end-points of the journey. So the structure and operation of our cities has a direct and measurable impact on community health. At the time of writing, those trends were still going in the wrong direction. In the year 2000, 2 per cent of Australian households had three or more vehicles; by 2009, the figure was 19 per cent. As many as 90 per cent of all journeys are now made by car. People are more likely to use public transport to get to work, but even there, about 80 per cent of commuters go by car. The example of urban living leads to the conclusion that we need to change a range of systems to accommodate legitimate aspirations while maintaining ecological integrity and improving social equity: 'climate-resilient infrastructure with low ecological footprint', mobility using less fossil fuels, 'meaningful work that doesn't erode quality of life, individual health or contributions to family and community', and systems that help people to recognise the broader impacts of their consumption choices.

In 2010, the Prime Minister's Science, Engineering and Innovation Council recommended we develop a national Resilient Cities and Towns Initiative 'to foster resilient, low-emission energy systems, water systems and built environment'. The idea was both to use tecÿological improvements to existing supply systems and to respond flexibly to the probable further increases in urban populations. This specific example illustrates the general conclusion of thinking about resilience. It is not an end in itself, but 'a perspective that can offer useful guidance at a system level'. A resilient society has more options for responding to outside pressures and unforeseen events. Given the uncertain future, we need structures that enable adaptability and learning from experience. Arguably, the recent electoral environment has encouraged dogmatic certainty and simplistic slogans, rather than a willingness to admit uncertainty and respond flexibly to policy initiatives which will inevitably be experimental. That is a critical impediment to the goal of creating a resilient Australia which will be able to adapt to the dramatic changes likely over the next few decades.

I was in the group that explored social and cultural factors influencing our future. Our work extended the resilience thinking by considering the social structures that affect our ability to respond to the changing biophysical environment. This led to worrying conclusions. We noted 'the confluence of biophysical and social factors' in peri-urban and regional areas where there are already social stresses and there are likely to be serious climate change impacts. We accepted the persuasive evidence that 'current patterns of spending and consumption, social organisation and structures' are not sustainable. Rather than ameliorating those trends, current policies are inexorably driving us toward an unsustainable future. So significant change is needed to achieve our stated goals of environmental and social sustainability.

In thinking about the biophysical world, serious studies have tried to identify what has been called a safe operating space: conditions which are consistent with our long-term survival. These studies show that we are now outside some of those boundaries, as discussed in earlier chapters; rapid climate change, human additions to the natural nitrogen cycle and accelerating loss of biodiversity are problems we need to deal with urgently, while increasing acidification of the oceans is also a serious worry. It is tempting to think that the same approach could be used to discuss social conditions, trying to identify the levels of inequity that would lead to social breakdown or the indicators of community well-being that indicate social stability. It has proved difficult if not impossible to apply that approach to society as a whole. We concluded that 'the social system is adaptable and resilient', while it is also true that 'people's perceptions about what is normal and acceptable also change'. That being said, we noted some warning signs of growing social tension in Australia: the increasing levels of long-term unemployment, housing insecurity and homelessness, decreasing civil engagement, rising incidence of chronic health conditions and increasing levels of violence. Subsequently, there was increasing concern in 2015 about the alarming number of victims of domestic violence, as well as public assaults by individuals who were both deranged and armed.

We concluded that developing a future which is both socially just and ecologically sustainable will require changes in values and attitudes. We all have to make choices consistent with that goal as well as electing leaders who put in place appropriate structures of rewards and penalties to facilitate those choices. Change is possible and most people are capable of making rational decisions if they are given good information. A classic Australian example is the process used by Douglas Shire in far north Queensland when faced with a problem of water quality. Their pristine water from the Daintree rainforest became polluted after land development and informal squatting, so the council realised they would need to begin treating the water supply to ensure it was safe to drink. The cheapest way to treat the water would have been chlorination, but this would have affected the shire's clean, green image which they considered vital to their tourist income. Cleaner technologies such as micro-filtration existed, but were much more expensive. Then mayor Mike Berwick recognised that either decision would have angered some of the community, so he took the wise step of involving the citizens. The council undertook engineering studies of four alternative technologies. Detailed reports were made available to the public and a simplified summary was distributed to every household, followed by a year of public discussion and a plebiscite in conjunction with the next council election. The community voted overwhelmingly for the cleanest but most expensive approach. Those who had other ideas were mollified because they had been given an opportunity to participate in the process. Overseas, a similar approach was used at the national level by Sweden to discuss its energy futures, involving the community in choices to implement the twin goals of reducing carbon dioxide releases while also phasing out nuclear power. By contrast, when the council in the Toowoomba area, in south-east Queensland, took a decision to introduce recycled water, it sparked a hostile campaign driven by local media which successfully opposed the initiative.

Much of the opposition was ill-informed and ignored the fact that most of the large cities of Europe use recycled water, but the process allowed them to carry the day.

Our group concluded that a productive way forward would be to develop a range of scenarios of possible futures, making it possible to involve the community in discussion of the alternatives. If we do have the broad conversation, discuss what 'the whole place is about' in Donald Horne's words, it will then be possible to make strategic decisions about population levels, urban development, transport, energy, food supply and so on, all within that agreed framework of our preferred future.

THINKING ABOUT FUTURES

There are various ways of thinking about futures. The most simplistic, often used by the commercial media, makes bold linear predictions, usually based on extrapolating past trends. For example, electricity prices have doubled in the past five years, therefore they will double in the next five. The Australian government once published predictions of future energy use, basically obtained by choosing almost at random an exponential growth factor and applying it to present use. The predictions were often out by 20 or 30 per cent, but they were specified with ridiculous precision. A better approach is to develop a range of projections, based on different assumptions. The Australian Bureau of Statistics takes this approach to population. It doesn't make forecasts but projections, each one based on specific assumptions about birthrate and migration levels. So they take the form, if current trends continue, the 2050 population will be 36 million, but if we adopt an approach of zero net migration, with the current birthrate it would be 28 million. The third and most sophisticated approach is to develop scenarios, credible stories of possible futures that allow their implications to be explored. As a specific example of this approach, one group working on the Academy of Science project developed three scenarios addressing the areas of response to climate change, governance and coping with complexity. In each case, they explored the benefits and risks of the approach.

In the Going for Growth scenario, Australian governments adopt an approach to our future development based on neoliberal economic principles, reducing regulation and promoting market-oriented solutions to emerging issues. In the short term, this might give the perceived benefit of continuing economic growth, as conventionally measured, with the possibility that some of this could flow down to improve the material living standards of the poor. A risk is that increasing inequality and declining environmental standards could worsen the existing trend of 'a disadvantaged underclass and considerable social tension'. In a second scenario they called Tax and Spend, governments use higher taxes to invest in health, education and welfare infrastructure as well as selective science initiatives. In this scenario, it would also be possible to use public funds for measures to improve social cohesion, such as community gardens and facilities for public occasions. A benefit would be better access to essential public services, while a risk would be the lower rate of economic growth leading to reduced capacity for private consumption. The third scenario, Post-materialism, envisaged governments setting broad parameters for environmental protection and implementing specific policies to stabilise population, limit overall energy use and cap the level of material production. The benefits could be better environmental quality and possibly a more socially harmonious society; the risk could be that reduced economic growth could limit our capacity to be adaptive in response to outside threats. The point of the exercise is that developing each scenario reveals the possible benefits as well as the possible negative outcomes, allowing a rational discussion of the alternatives.

I was involved in a similar exercise on a much smaller scale when my local council on the Sunshine Coast ran a community process in 2003–04 to explore alternative futures for our region. Groups considered specific issues such as transport, urban development, employment, education and so on. Their work flowed together into a broader discussion of four scenarios for the future of the region. A startling level of consensus emerged. At the final gathering of about 1,000 residents, there was nearly 90 per cent support for one scenario. It limited the growth of the region, maintaining areas of natural vegetation and providing good public transport between compact urban villages, an approach which put quality of life and environmental protection ahead of expansion and economic growth. The citizens who took part were disappointed and disillusioned when the local council continued on its trajectory of rapid growth; the voters showed their anger at the subsequent election by removing many of the elected representatives. The council survivors seem to have learned their lesson; in 2015, a proposed high-rise development on the coast was rejected after strong community opposition.

The second phase of the Academy of Science project brought together 50 Australians from diverse backgrounds in 2013 to discuss the reports and work together defining possible futures for Australia. What is particularly significant, given the disparate group involved in that meeting, is what the report called 'a widely-held [sic] preference for the future'. It consists of 'a future Australia that is more caring, community-focused and fair than present-day Australia'. These 50 Australians took turns to discuss four types of possible futures under the headings of Growth, Restraint, Catastrophe and Transformation.

Growth 'was considered more broadly than just economic growth. Positive futures … involved growth in human wellbeing and engagement. Such futures were thought to depend on growth in terms of helpful advances in health, social and cultural diversity, democratic engagement and technologies helping people manage information … Many potentially undesirable aspects of growth futures were identified, including exceeding resource limits, inequity, social exclusion and the stress of dealing with a dependence on ever-changing technologies.' Discussion of this possible future recognised that 'a culture of consumerism' is currently driving economic growth. The pursuit of growth as measured by GDP is likely to be encouraged by the present trend of globalisation, accentuated by neoliberal economic theories and new trade agreements. The groups recognised that the Australian population will inevitably continue to grow for at least a few decades, even longer if current policies persist, with serious negative consequences, especially for urban areas where recent growth has been concentrated. They thought 'inclusive and equitable governance' would be needed for growth to continue without serious social divisions, and were concerned that an emphasis on growth could inadvertently produce disastrous outcomes: 'domestic or international conflicts and/or destruction caused by inappropriate growth'.

Restraint was seen as 'a prudent response to awareness of future limits to aspects of our lifestyles (e.g. limits to availability of natural resources, how much stress people can absorb, or how much inequality a society finds acceptable) … it was envisaged that a society that does anticipate and prepare could steer Australia to an active, healthy and happy future – with perhaps less diversity of material products but greater wellbeing'. Such futures were seen to be technically feasible and socially desirable, putting greater value on the common good and on overall well-being than on wealth accumulation. Desirable changes could include 'more local production and distribution of food, increased eating of food in season, and reduced consumption of meat and processed foods'. Though these sorts of futures were judged to have many advantages, the group thought them unlikely given current social norms. Restraint could be forced on us by scarcity or adversity, and the group recognised that 'people accept restraint when faced with adversity'. A critical point is that restraint can be an acceptable approach only if it applies to all: 'restraint will not happen without widespread support'. A good example is the rationing of food and fuel in the UK during World War II. Because it was applied equally and was directed toward a widely supported desirable outcome, the restraint was generally accepted. The discussion also accepted the political reality that 'cycles that favour short-term outcomes and planning horizons are a significant hindrance' to that sort of future.

For Catastrophe, 'there are many and varied possibilities. Shocks and emergencies are typical triggers for catastrophes, but their impact ... depends on how prepared society is for them.' The group considered a range of possible catastrophic events, local ones such as fires or floods, national ones such as food insecurity or water shortages, global ones such as disease pandemics or mass migration of refugees, as is already occurring. Conflicts arising from inequality or the collapse of support systems were also discussed. The obvious conclusion was that these sorts of futures 'feature low quality of life for most ... little happiness, high unemployment, no leisure, overcrowded conditions, high levels of violence and homelessness, and growing uncertainty and insecurity in damaged ecosystems and urban environments'. The report continued:

While the above reads like a catalogue of horrors, it allows us to think about how to avoid or at least prepare for undesirable futures. Valuable contributions to adaptive capacity include insurance systems, well-maintained critical infrastructure, a portfolio of alternative sources of energy and resources, risk assessment and planning, a precautionary approach to ecosystem management, building resilient supply chains, good leadership and governance, and a culture that values learning. It was concluded that anticipating change, preparing for it and learning from experience are essential elements of the ability to cope with shocks.

Transformation was interpreted in terms of cultural change to be 'truly diverse, respectful and equitable', technological change in health care and access to information, and governance changes toward 'community-driven decision making'. Two factors that were seen as 'particularly powerful catalysts for transformational change between now and 2050' were 'wider consideration of what Australians want and what progress we are making towards those goals, and stronger incentives for desirable policies and actions'. The group recognised that we talk about transformation quite routinely when we discuss tax reform, law reform or adopting new technologies like mobile phones. Transformation can be a result of our conscious decisions, as when we set a renewable energy target or adopt a so-called free trade agreement, or can be imposed on us by forces we do not directly control such as global climate change or international conflict. Many thought that 'an Australia with high levels of fairness, tolerance and caring, based on a sustainable relationship with the natural environment' would amount to a transformation rather than an evolution from the current situation. 'If Australians want to have a say about if and how the nation transforms, it might require (1) recognition across society that major change is needed, (2) having and sharing ideas about how to make that change, and (3) social acceptance of that change.' So the group concluded that we would benefit from 'processes that encourage society-wide dialogue about our beliefs, hopes and aspirations, our relationship with nature, learning lessons from Australia's past and from the rest of the world, and harnessing our collective imagination about what Australia could be'.

While considering these extremes is a useful strategy to extend our thinking, the real future is likely to be some sort of mixture rather than one coherent scenario. Some common observations emerged from discussing these future possibilities. One was that 'achieving desired futures might require a large degree of change, perhaps fundamental change'. 'While recognising that there are many desirable aspects of current Australia, many participants pointed to undesirable levels of inequality in various forms, including inequality of wealth, education, health and life opportunities, and intolerance of cultural and other diversity.' There was also general concern about environmental degradation and resource exploitation, but 'differing opinions about their urgency'. A third common understanding was that 'society's choices might have a bigger impact on the future than many participants previously thought'. That is a critical point. Politicians often speak in terms of a future that they see unrolling inexorably as the inevitable consequence of economic trends. We do have choices, and those choices will determine which mix of the possible futures actually takes place. But several of the participants expressed concern about 'current governance arrangements and their ability to prepare Australia for an uncertain future', specifying 'declining trust in government', the lack of a shared vision guiding policy and even the fundamental question of whether our current democratic system allows long-term planning. I agree that this is at least as serious a problem in 2016 as when Donald Horne lamented the shortcomings of our leaders. The fixation with neoliberal economic models has almost made planning a dirty word in government circles, replaced by a ridiculous faith that the magic of the market will produce the best possible future. Even Adam Smith recognised in 1776 that the market needs to be regulated if it is to produce socially beneficial outcomes. Governments wedded to the extreme neoliberal approach, such as the Key administration in New Zealand and some Coalition governments in Australia, have effectively removed the notion of sustainability from their discussions, as if recognising that it shines an embarrassing light on their short-sighted approach. The future is a very unwelcome guest at the neoliberal banquet.

Perhaps the most basic conclusion of the whole Academy of Science exercise was that we need leadership and good governance to enable Australians to think about their preferred future 'and build a national culture of preparing for multiple challenges and opportunities'. On the other hand, 'pathways to catastrophe futures mostly involve poor leadership and governance, lack of anticipation or preparation for change ...' This is a chilling reminder of what Donald Horne said about our leaders. There is no evidence that the quality of leadership is better today than it was in 1964. While there might have been some excuse for ignorance 50 years ago, the evidence that we are living beyond our means is now inescapable. Only leaders blinded by ideology could still be pursuing growth as the primary goal and ignoring the clear evidence emerging of the inevitable consequences of their decisions.

GETTING THE BALANCE RIGHT

In his 2014 book *Northern Lights: The Positive Policy Examples of Sweden, Finland, Denmark and Norway*, Andrew Scott pointed out that 'the four main Nordic nations have achieved much lower levels of child poverty, better supports and services for parents when their children are young, better work/life balance, better school results, greater skills and opportunities for workers still in their prime working years, and a sounder base of revenue for necessary government spending, including on environmental measures, than have been achieved in Australia and other English-speaking countries'. He notes that these outcomes are not accidental, but the result of conscious policies that have a better balance between the economic, the social and the environmental policies. This is consistent with the finding I mentioned earlier, that those four countries occupied the top four places in the UN 2015 assessment of progress toward sustainability. Satyajit Das shows in *A Banquet of Consequences* that assuming all our problems can be solved by economic growth, as most politicians do, does not even make sense within the narrow framework of economics. We are now in a new economic era, with the capacity for continuing growth obviously constrained by resource limits and accumulating environmental problems. As the World Economic Forum noted in 2008, we desperately need a new overall approach.

About 20 years ago, I saw the then NSW premier, Bob Carr, argue that we needed to get the balance right between economic, social and environmental issues. He illustrated his talk with a diagram showing the three domains as being of equal size and importance. I commented that most decision-makers actually work to something more like what I have called the pig-headed model, shown in Figure 1: the economy is dominant, like the pig's face, with social and environmental questions seen as minor areas like the pig's ears. We will make progress only when we recognise the reality that the economy is just a means to an end of greater human welfare, and is therefore a subsection of our society. Our social organisations are in turn located within the natural systems of this finite planet. That world view was really established in the 1960s when we saw the Earth from space for the first time. Looking at the planet as a whole, we see the perilously thin membrane that supports life and the physical features that we use to mark national boundaries. There is no sign of 'the economy' or 'the market', these artificial constructs that get so much time every night in news bulletins. That perspective gives an organisational approach represented by Figure 2, the view from space or the 'eco-nested' model. We have the prospect of a sustainable future only if our decision-makers recognise this reality: our social structure must exist within the framework of natural ecological systems, and our economic planning must recognise that social context.

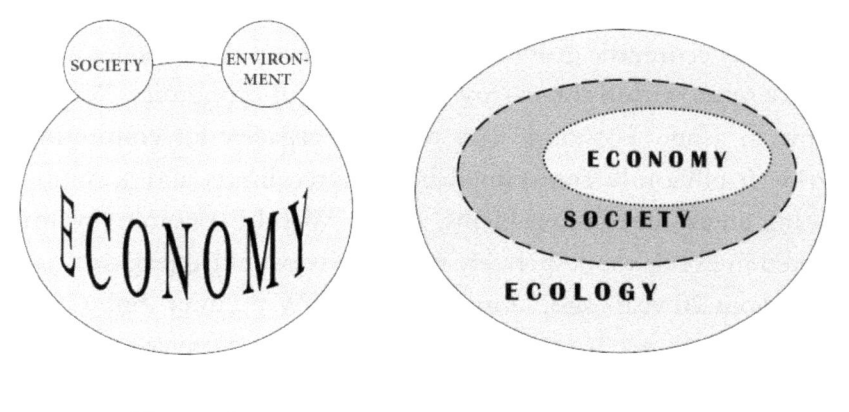

Figure 1

Figure 2

I set out in *A Big Fix: Radical Solutions for Australia's Environmental Crisis* the general attributes of a sustainable society. It is a simple checklist:

- It will have a stable population that is using resources at a rate that is sustainable.
- It will be approaching the goal of zero waste.
- As well as being committed to maintaining the natural areas that exist, it will also be restoring some of the natural assets that have been lost or degraded in earlier times.
- It will be a low-carbon society, meeting its energy needs from a mix of renewable technologies, principally wind and solar.
- It will be much more equitable than today's society, reducing the pressure to expand consumption levels.
- We will have a more mature politics, with an inclusive process for making difficult decisions, recognising that you can never change only one thing in a complex system, so change always has losers as well as winners.

The most important principle to recognise is that the future is not somewhere we are going; it is something we are creating. At any given time, there are many possible futures. Which one eventuates will be the product of our choices and actions, individually and as groups. It will, of course, be influenced by global events over which we have no control. We should be aware of the old sailing maxim: we cannot choose which wind will blow, but we can set the sails. A good sailor can use whatever wind is blowing to head in the direction they choose. Recognising the global forces we cannot control does not imply meekly surrendering our fate to those forces. As Donald Horne said, we have the resources and the qualities to do better and become a great nation, an exemplar to others as they face the same existential crisis as is facing us. The choice is ours.

It is always tempting to concentrate on the short term and enjoy the wonderful privilege of living in modern Australia. We live more comfortably than any previous generation, we are healthier, we live longer, we have opportunities for travel and different experiences that no humans have ever had before. But we also have a responsibility to recognise that we are literally consuming the resources that our own descendants will need, changing the global climate which will impact them directly, reducing the biological diversity on which they will depend, and reinforcing social inequality which will reduce the chances of them having a secure future. With privilege comes responsibility. We have been privileged to enjoy the fruits of the work of previous generations of Australians. We are now responsible for the world our descendants will inherit. Working together, we can make it a better world.

ACKNOWLEDGEMENTS

When Alexandra Payne of University of Queensland Press asked me if I was considering writing another book, I immediately thought of revisiting Donald Horne's wonderful contribution to our thinking about Australia. The Independent Scholars Association of Australia decided to make the theme of their 2014 conference *The Lucky Country Fifty Years On*, so I offered a paper in which I gave preliminary consideration to some of the ideas I have developed in this book. My thinking was greatly clarified by the discussion at that conference and my interaction with Nick and Julia Horne, Donald's children, as well as a diverse group of scholars with critical reflections on the ideas in *The Lucky Country*. The arguments in this book have been refined by discussions with students and colleagues over the years. It has been, as always, a real pleasure to work with Alexandra Payne and Kristy BusYell at University of Queensland Press. Nikki Lusk did a wonderful job of editing the manuscript, not just improving my expression but also proposing structural changes that made this a much better book.

I have been supported in the task of writing by my wonderful life partner, Dr Patricia Kelly. The book has been improved out of sight by her insightful comments on the draft manuscript.

More importantly, her love and companionship over the years we have shared has made me the person who could write a book like this.

SOURCES

Appadurai, Arjun, 'Disjuncture and Difference in the Global Cultural Economy', *Theory, Culture and Society*, vol. 7, 1990, pp. 295–310.

Archer, Colin & Annette Willi, *Opportunity Costs: Military Spending and the UN's Development Agenda*, International Peace Bureau, Zurich, 2012.

Australian Bureau of Statistics, *Measures of Australia's Progress*, cat. no. 137.0, ABS, Canberra, 2013.

Australian Government, Department of Agriculture, *Australian Fisheries and Aquaculture Statistics 2013*, Canberra, 2014, available at data.daff.gov.au/data/warehouse/9aam/afstad9aamd003/2013/AustFishAquacStats_2013_v1.2.0.pdf.

Beresford, Quentin, *The Rise and Fall of Gunns Ltd*, NewSouth Books, Sydney, 2015.

Beyond Zero Emissions, *Zero Carbon Australia Stationary Energy Plan*, BZE, Melbourne, 2010.

BHP Billiton, *Olympic Dam Expansion Draft Environmental Impact Statement*, BHP Billiton, Melbourne, 2009.

Birch, Charles, *Confronting the Future: Australia and the World: The Next Hundred Years*, Penguin, Melbourne, 1975.

Birrell, Robert, Doug Hill & JoŸ Stanley, *Quarry Australia?* Oxford University Press, Melbourne, 1982.

Bryant, Nick, *The Rise and Fall of Australia*, Random House, North Sydney, 2014.

Church, Norman, 'Why Our Food is so Dependent on Oil', Powerswitch, 2005, available at resilience.org/stories/2005-04-01/why-our-food-so-dependent-oil.

Commonwealth of Australia, *Compendium of Ecologically Sustainable Development Recommendations*, Canberra, 1992.

Cork, Steven, Nicky Grigg, Kristin Alford, JoŸ Finnigan, Beth Fulton & Michael Raupach, *Australia 2050: Structuring Conversations about Our Future*, Australian Academy of Science, Canberra, 2015.

Council of Australian Governments, *National Strategy for Ecologically Sustainable Development*, Canberra, 1992, available at environment.gov.au/about-us/esd/publications/national-esd-strategy.

Cribb, Julian, *The Coming Famine: The Global Food Crisis and What We Can Do to Avoid It*, CSIRO Publishing, Clayton, 2010.

Czech, Brian, *Supply Shock: Economic Growth at the Crossroads and the Steady State Solution*, New Society Publishers, Gabriola Island, Canada, 2013.

Daly, Herman E, *Beyond Growth: The Economics of Sustainable Development*, Beacon Press, Boston, 1996.

Das, Satyajit, *A Banquet of Consequences*, Penguin, Melbourne, 2015.

Davis, Glyn, 'The Endless Seminar', *Griffith Review*, issue 28, 2010, pp. 130–61.

Diesendorf, Mark, *Greenhouse Solutions with Sustainable Energy*, 2nd edition, UNSW Press, Sydney, 2014.

Dorsey, Michael, 'Conversations with Great Minds, with Thom Hartmann', 2014, available at conversationswithgreatminds.com/video/conversations-great-minds-p1-dr-michael-dorsey-social-justice-climate-policy.

Dotto, Lydia & Harold Schiff, *The Ozone War*, Doubleday, New York, 1978.

Elliston, Ben, Iain MacGill & Mark Diesendorf, 'Comparing Least-cost Scenarios for 100% Renewable Electricity with Low Emission Fossil Fuel Scenarios in the Australian National Electricity Market', *Renewable Energy*, vol. 66, 2014, pp. 196–204.

Food and Agriculture Organization of the United Nations, *The State of the World Fisheries and Aquaculture*, FAO, Rome, 2014.

Friedrichs, Jörg, *The Future Is Not What It Used to Be: Climate Change and Energy Scarcity*, The MIT Press, Cambridge, MA, 2013.

Gittins, Ross, *The Happy Economist: Happiness for the Hard-headed*, Allen & Unwin, Crows Nest, 2010.

Gleeson-White, Jane, *Six Capitals*, Allen & Unwin, Crows Nest, 2014.

Goldie, Jenny & Katharine Betts (eds), *Sustainable Futures: Linking Population, Resources and the Environment*, CSIRO Publishing, Collingwood, 2014.

Sources

Gore, Al, *An Inconvenient Truth: The Planetary Emergency of Global Warming and What We Can Do About It*, Rodale Press, Emmaus, Pennsylvania, 2006.

Green, Maurice B, *Eating Oil: Energy Use in Food Production*, Westview Press, Boulder, Colorado, 1978.

Heinberg, Richard, *The End of Growth: Adapting to Our New Economic Reality*, New Society Publishers, Gabriola Island, Canada, 2011.

Higgs, Kerryn, *Collision Course: Endless Growth on a Finite Planet*, The MIT Press, Cambridge, MA, 2014.

Hinckley, Elias, 'Historic Moment: Saudi Arabia Sees End of Oil Age Coming and Opens Valve on the Carbon Bubble', *Energy Post*, 22 January 2015, available at energypost.eu/historic-moment-saudi-arabia-sees-end-oil-age-coming-opens-valves-carbon-bubble.

Horne, Donald, *The Lucky Country*, Penguin, Melbourne, 1964.

—— *The Lucky Country*, fifth edition, Penguin, Melbourne, 1998.

—— *Think or Perish: Towards a Confident and Productive Australia*, Questioning the future occasional paper: no. 8, Australian Government Publishing Service for Commission for the Future, Carlton, 1988.

Hunt, Tam, 'The Future of the Electric Car', *greentechgrid*, 1 April 2015, available at greentechmedia.com/articles/read/the-future-of-the-electric-car.

Hussain, Dilly, 'ISIS: The "Unintended Consequences" of the US-led War on Iraq', *Foreign Policy Journal*, 23 March 2015, availableatforeignpolicyjournal.com/2015/03/23/isis-the-unintended-consequences-of-the-us-led-war-on-iraq/.

Independent Scholars Association of Australia, *The Lucky Country Fifty Years On*, 2014 Conference Proceedings, ISAA, Canberra, 2015.

International Energy Agency, *World Energy Outlook 2014*, IEA, Paris, 2014.

International Integrated Reporting Council, *Capitals: Background Paper for <IR>*, theiirc.org, 2013.

Jones, Barry, *Sleepers, Wake! Tecÿology and the Future of Work*, Oxford University Press, Melbourne, 1982.

Kelly, Patricia, *Towards Globo Sapiens: Transforming Learners in Higher Education*, Sense Publishers, Rotterdam, 2008.

Kevin, Tony, *Crunch Time: Using and Abusing Keynes to Fight the Twin Crises of Our Era*, Scribe Publications, Carlton North, 2009.

King, Jonathan, *Waltzing Materialism*, fifth printing, Harper and Row, Sydney, 1984.

Klein, Naomi, *This Changes Everything: Capitalism vs. the Climate*, Simon & Schuster Paperbacks, New York, 2014.

Leigh, Andrew, *Battlers and Billionaires*, Black Inc., Melbourne, 2013.

Lloyd's, *Food System Shock: The Insurance Impacts of Acute Disruption to Global Food Supply*, Emerging Risk Report, 2015, available at lloyds.com/~/media/files/news%20and%20insight/risk%20insight/2015/food%20system%20shock/food%20system%20shock_exec%20summary_june%202015.pdf.

Lo Bianco, Joseph & Yvette Slaughter, *Second Languages and Australian Schooling*, ACER Press, Camberwell, 2009.

Lowe, Ian, *Living in the Greenhouse*, Scribe Publications, Newham, 1989.

—— 'Spend for a Healthier Future', in Bronwen Levy & Ffion Murphy (eds), *Story/telling*, University of Queensland Press, St Lucia, 2001.

—— *Living in the Hothouse: How Global Warming Affects Australia*, Scribe Publications, Carlton, 2005.

—— *A Big Fix: Radical Solutions for Australia's Environmental Crisis* 2nd edition, Black Inc., Melbourne, 2009.

—— *Bigger or Better? Australia's Population Debate*, University of Queensland Press, St Lucia, 2012.

Manne, Robert, '*Laudato si*': a political reading', *The Monthly*, 1 July 2015, available at themonthly.com.au/blog/robert-manne/2015/01/2015/1435708320/laudato-si-political-reading.

Marmot, Michael, *The Health Gap: The Challenge of an Unequal World*, Bloomsbury, London, 2015.

Mason, Paul, *Postcapitalism: A Guide to Our Future*, Allen Lane, London, 2015.

—— 'The End of Captialism Has Begun', *The Guardian*, 17 July 2015, theguardian.com/books/2015/jul/17/postcapitalism-end-of-capitalism-begun.

Meadows, Dennis, Donella Meadows, Jørgen Randers & William W Behrens III, *The Limits to Growth: A Report for the Club of Rome's Project on the Predicament of Mankind*, Universe Books, New York, 1972.

Millennium Ecosystem Assessment, *Ecosystems and Human Well-being: Synthesis*, Island Press, Washington, DC, 2005.

Milne, Seumas, 'Now the Truth Emerges: How the US Fuelled the Rise of ISIS in Syria and Iraq', *The Guardian*, 4 June 2015, available at theguardian.com/commentisfree/2015/jun/03/us-isis-syria-iraq.

Monbiot, George, 'The Insatiable God', *The Guardian*, 18 November 2014, available at monbiot.com/2014/11/18/the-insatiable-god/.

Sources

Muenzel, Valentin, Iven Mareels & Julian de Hoog, 'Affordable Batteries for Green Energy are Closer than We Think', *The Conversation*, 23 July 2014, available at theconversation.com/affordable-batteries-for-green-energy-are-closer-than-we-think-28772.

National Framework for Energy Efficiency, *Final Report*, Australian Government, Canberra, 2003.

Newman, Peter & Jeffrey Kenworthy, *Sustainability and Cities: Overcoming Automobile Dependence*, Island Press, Washington, DC, 1999.

Pedersen, Peder Vejsig, Jakob Klint, Karin Kappel & Katrine Vejsig Pedersen, *Green Solar Cities*, Earthscan, London, 2015.

Pope Francis, *Laudato Si'*, 2015, available at w2.vatican.va/content/dam/francesco/pdf/encyclicals/documents/papa-francesco_20150524_enciclica-laudato-si_en.pdf.

Ranger Uranium Environmental Inquiry, *First Report*, Australian Government Printing Service, Canberra, 1976.

Raskin, Paul D, *The Great Transition Today: A Report from the Future*, essay #2 in the GTI Paper Series *Frontiers of a Great Transition*, Tellus Institute, Boston, 2006.

—— Tariq Banuri, Gilberto Gallopin, Pablo Gutman, Al Hammond, Robert Kates & Rob Swart, *Great Transition: The Promise and Lure of the Times Ahead*, A report of the Global Scenario Group, Tellus Institute, Boston, 2002.

Raupach, Michael R, Anthony J McMichael, JoŸ J Finnigan, Lenore Manderson & Brian H Walker (eds), *Negotiating our Future: Living Scenarios for Australia to 2050*, Australian Academy of Science, Canberra, 2012.

Rogers, JoŸ, 'And the Cheapest Electricity in the US is … Solar', *Renew Economy*, 17 July 2015, available at reneweconomy.com.au/2015/and-the-cheapest-electricity-in-the-us-is-solar-52098.

Scott, Andrew, *Northern Lights: The Positive Policy Example of Sweden, Finland, Denmark and Norway*, Monash University Publishing, Clayton, 2014.

Sipe, Neil & Karen Vella (eds), *Australian Handbook of Urban and Regional Planning*, Routledge, London, forthcoming.

Smith, Adam, *An Inquiry into the Nature and Causes of the Wealth of Nations*, Strahan and Cadell, London, 1776.

State of the Environment Advisory Council, *Australia: State of the Environment 1996*, CSIRO Publishing, Collingwood, 1996.

State of the Environment 2011 Committee, *Australia State of the*

Environment 2011, Independent Report to the Australian Government Minister for Sustainability, Environment, Water, Population and Communities, DSEWPaC, Canberra, 2011.

The Lancet, 'Health and Climate Change: Policy Responses to Protect Human Health', 23 June 2015, available at thelancet.com/commissions/climate-change-2015.

—— 'Safeguarding Human Health in the Anthropocene Epoch: Report of the Rockefeller Foundation – Lancet Commission on Planetary Health', 16 July 2015, available at thelancet.com/commissions/planetary-health.

UNEP, *Global Environmental Outlook 3*, Earthscan Publications, London, 2002.

—— *Global Environmental Outlook 5*, 2012, available at unep.org/geo/geo5.asp.

UNICEF, 'Military Expenditure: The Opportunity Cost', 2000, available at unicef.org/sowc96/8mlitary.htm.

Victor, Peter, *Managing without Growth: Slower by Design, Not Disaster*, Edward Elgar Publishing, Cheltenham, 2008.

Washington, Haydn, *Addicted to Growth?*, CASSE NSW, Sydney, 2014.

—— *Demystifying Sustainability: Towards Real Solutions*, Routledge, London, 2015.

Weiss, Linda, Elizabeth Thurbon & JoŸ Mathews, *How to Kill a Country: Australia's Devastating Trade Deal with the United States*, Allen & Unwin, Crows Nest, 2004.

White, Hugh, *Power Shift: Australia's Future Between Washington and Beijing*, Quarterly Essay 39, Black Inc., Melbourne, 2010.

Williams, Roy, *Post-God Nation? How Religion Fell Off the Radar in Australia – and What Might be Done To Get It Back On*, HarperCollins Publishers, Sydney, 2015.

World Commission on Environment and Development, *Our Common Future*, United Nations, 1987.

World Economic Forum, *Summit on the Global Agenda*, WEF, Geneva, 2014.

WWF International, *Living Planet Report 2014*, World Wide Fund for Nature, Gland, Switzerland, 2014.

Yencken, David & Debra Wilkinson, *Resetting the Compass: Australia's Journey Towards Sustainability*, CSIRO Publishing, Collingwood, 2000.